Systems Lifecycle Cost-Effectiveness

Systems Lifecycle Cost-Effectiveness

The Commercial, Design and Human Factors of Systems Engineering

MASSIMO PICA

Routledge
Taylor & Francis Group

LONDON AND NEW YORK

First published in paperback 2024

First published 2014 by Ashgate Publishing

Published 2016 by Routledge
4 Park Square, Milton Park, Abingdon, Oxon OX14 4RN

and by Routledge
605 Third Avenue, New York, NY 10158

Routledge is an imprint of the Taylor & Francis Group, an informa business

British Library Cataloguing in Publication Data
A catalogue record for this book is available from the British Library

Library of Congress Cataloging-in-Publication Data
Pica, Massimo.
 Systems lifecycle cost-effectiveness : the commercial, design, and human factors of systems engineering / by Massimo Pica.
  pages cm
 Includes bibliographical references and index.
 ISBN 978-1-4094-6246-0 (hardback) -- ISBN 978-1-4094-6247-7 (ebook) -- ISBN 978-1-4094-6248-4 (epub) 1. Systems engineering--Cost effectiveness. 2. Product life cycle. I. Title. II. Title: Systems life cycle cost-effectiveness.
 TA168.P48 2014
 620.0068'5--dc23

2013035195

ISBN: 978-1-4094-6246-0 (hbk)
ISBN: 978-1-03-283750-5 (pbk)
ISBN: 978-1-315-61173-0 (ebk)

DOI: 10.4324/9781315611730

Contents

PART ONE: BASIC CONCEPTS

PART TWO: DETAILED APPROACH – SELECTED APPLICATIONS

List of Figures

List of Tables

List of Abbreviations

A	Constant annual payment
A_O	Operational Availability
ABC	Activity Based Costing
ABLCC	Activity Based Life Cycle Costing
C	Capability
CADRe	Cost Analysis Data Requirement
CBS	Cost Breakdown Structure
C_C	Unit cost for Concept Stage
C_D	Unit cost for Development Stage
CER	Cost Estimating Relationship
C_{mn}	Cost elements of Life Cycle Cost
C_N	Equivalent cost for a new system
COCOMO	Constructive Cost Model
COSOSIMO	Constructive System-of-Systems Integration Cost Model
COSYSMO	Constructive Systems Engineering Cost Model
COTS	Commercial off the Shelf

C_P	Non recurring and first unit production cost of a previous system
C_p	Unit cost for Production Stage
DCF	Discounted Cash Flow
D_O	Operational Dependability
DM	Direct material cost
f	Annual inflation rate
F	Current money amount
F_C	Complexity factor ratio
F_M	Miniaturization factor ratio
F_P	Productivity component ratio
F_1	First annual payment in a cash flow series
FOM	Figure of Merit
FP	Function Points
g	Uniform percentage variation of annual payments
G	Uniform variation of annual payments
HFs	Human Factors
HMI	Human Machine Interface
HSI	Human Systems Integration
i	Interest rate or discounting rate inclusive of inflation
i'	Interest rate or discounting rate neglecting the inflation

ICT	Information and Communication Technology
IEA	International Ergonomics Association
IEC	International Electrotechnical Commission
INCOSE	International Council on Systems Engineering
IRR	Internal Rate of Return
ISO	International Organization for Standardization
ISP	Integrated Support Plan
K£	Thousand GB Pounds
KPP	Key Performance Parameter
LC	Learning Curve
LCC	Life Cycle Cost
LCCA	Unit acquisition cost
LCCO	Unit ownership cost[1]
LCCR	Unit retirement cost[2]
LORA	Level of Repair Analysis
LR	Labour Rate
m	Cost element category subscript
M	Maximum value of m
MIS	Management Information System

---

1 Abbreviations of ownership cost sub-elements are omitted
2 Abbreviations of retirement cost sub-elements are omitted

MOE	Measure of Effectiveness
MOP	Measure of Performance
MTBF	Mean time between consecutive failures
MTTR	Mean time to repair
M£	Million GB Pounds
n	Number of years in economic analysis
N	Maximum value of n
NDI	Non Developmental Items
NPV	Net Present Value
OH	Overhead cost
P	Constant money amount
PV	Present Value
RAMS	Reliability, Availability, Maintainability, Supportability
RMP	Risk Management Plan
SE	System Effectiveness
SLOC	Source Lines of Code
SoS	System-of-Systems
SRR	System Requirements Review
STTE	Special-to-Type Test Equipment
TPM	Technical Performance Measure

t_n Average unit production time in a series of n units

t_{2n} Average unit production time in a series of 2n units

WBS   Work Breakdown Structure

WLC   Whole Life Cost

Foreword

Arthur Griffiths
Past Chairman
Society for Cost Analysis and Forecasting

During my years as a managing consultant and Chairman of the Society for Cost Analysis and Forecasting I have come to recognize the major problems involved with evaluating cost-effective systems that also achieve best value for money.

'Cost is a consequence of design'. This often used phrase would be heard on many occasions during decision making meetings on major capital investment projects. Various engineers and cost analysts would be left to fight their corners, each attempting to agree on optimum solutions for the system options being considered.

I am delighted to see a book that combines and addresses the issues of system engineering, cost analysis and economics. The book not only provides an understanding of the basic concepts of system engineering and life cycle costs but leads on with worked examples for practical applications and knowledge transfer.

It is particularly pleasing to see that as well as system engineering and cost aspects, the text stresses the importance of management, design, human factors and commercial considerations and illustrates how they should be addressed.

The task of developing and delivering capital intensive complex engineering projects has probably never been more difficult for engineers and managers particularly in the areas of mitigating potential life cycle cost growth while achieving cost-effective system optimization. With political pressure to minimize expenditure and the drive for value for money with shrinking resources it is essential that people involved today in the delivery of complex projects understand the wide range of often conflicting issues and interests which affect project acquisition.

This book contains comprehensive text that can be used by the student, experienced system engineers, cost analysts and managers alike to improve their understanding of the wide range of issues involved in the evaluation of system life cycle cost-effectiveness.

Foreword

Marcel Smit
Senior Research Scientist
TNO, Delft, The Netherlands

The topic system life cycle cost effectiveness becomes more and more important these days. In a time where budgets are cut, new and existing systems have to perform optimally with the lowest possible costs.

However, maximizing the system effectiveness and at the same time minimizing the costs are two conflicting objectives. Therefore, optimizing the system life cycle cost effectiveness is a very complex matter with many factors of influence.

This book covers all the possible factors of influence on the system effectiveness and on the life cycle costs. In the book the theory of the basic concepts is described. Besides this essential theoretical background, the book also provides the practical elaborations in a number of selected applications, illustrating the theory of the first part of the book. The second part also provides for some subjects in more mathematical depth.

Massimo Pica has used his experience of more than 30 years as a professional engineer in the Italian Army to write this practical book. I know Massimo from a number of international working groups on Life Cycle Costs. Although we have completely different scientific backgrounds: he is a chemical engineer and I am an econometrician, we both share the same interest in the valuable combination of science and economics. This interest eventually led to writing this book.

Massimo has contributed to two NATO Research and Technology Organization working groups that I chaired: SAS-054 – Methods and Models for Life Cycle Costs, and SAS-069 – Code of Practice for Life Cycle Costing. We also cooperated in a NATO working group developing the first Allied

Publication on Life Cycle Costs (ALCCP-1) – Guidance on Life Cycle Costs and we both participated for a number of years in a NATO working group on a specific system of systems development: NATO Cost Analysis Team on Missile Defence.

Although most experience was built up in the defence and security environment, the topics discussed in this book are very broadly targeted and can be applied in any environment dealing with capital intensive goods. This makes the book very useful and helpful in all industries, so, I would like to recommend it to those who are working on any engineering, development and maintenance project and wish to know more about system life cycle cost effectiveness, together with students and managers will also gain benefit from the book.

Preface
Technology, Innovations and the Human Side of Systems

There is nothing more difficult to take in hand, more perilous to conduct, or more uncertain in its success, than to take the lead in the introduction of a new order of things: in fact the innovator has for enemies all those who have done well under the old conditions, and lukewarm defenders in those who may do well under the new.

N. Machiavelli (Florence 1469–1527), 'The Prince'

Systems Life Cycle Management and Operational/Commercial Opportunities in an Era of Technological Innovations

Technological innovations (from the Latin word *innovare* which means that something new – *novus* – is introduced into an existing system) imply the concept of improvement.

For an improvement to take place, people have to change the way they make decisions, or to make different choices. According to a statement attributed to J.A. Schumpeter, *'innovation changes the values onto which the system is based'*. On the basis of the theory of *'Creative Destruction'*, proposed by Schumpeter, Alan Greenspan said: *'One result of the more-rapid pace of the technology innovation has been a visible acceleration of the process of creative destruction, that is the shifting of capital from falling, mature technologies into those technologies at the cutting edge.'*

Today, the world economy is strongly dependent on innovation, from a sound scientific perspective. Inventions are being converted into innovative systems, products and services for the present and future benefits to society. As Albert Einstein said, *'Let's not pretend that things will change if we keep doing the same things'*.

Conversely, whenever a change is deriving from innovations to cause improvements, it should be taken into account that, as the English sixteenth-century theologian Richard Hooker wrote, *'change is not made without inconvenience, even from worse to better'*. Technological innovations of systems of interest both to engineers and to relevant user communities often mean that the projects launched to make these systems available are also becoming more and more complex, as well as challenging from the economic point of view. On the other hand, as recently pointed out by Dr Callum Kidd of the University of Manchester, *'the ability to change faster and more efficiently/cost effectively is now an imperative, not a target'*.

Therefore, it is recommended that the capability to analyze, synthesize and design complex systems be properly preserved in acquisition programmes. Designing a system is a multi-variate challenge, involving composite decision-making processes in the selection among different solutions complying with the same specifications in order to achieve an adequate performance level for the delivered system. This kind of decision is in most cases dictated by cost-effectiveness considerations, taking primarily into account the correlation between the compliance to the system total cost requirements and objectives and schedule constraints in correspondence to an acceptable risk level.

As noted by Farr in his book (Farr, 2011), *'true systems costing must be better tied to real systems engineering issues like integration and costing. Also we need to better understand how to relate architecture to costing. Systems are now designed using architecture and complex modeling languages such as SysML'*.

In general, it should absolutely be emphasized that technological innovations characterizing advanced systems require a careful balance of the whole acquisition, ownership, and retirement costs, encompassed in the Life Cycle Cost, in order to avoid unjustified trends in cost growth.

The problem of cost growth for system acquisition programmes has been troublesome for decades, specifically in the defence sector but actually with a more general meaning for broader categories of assets. There are several factors potentially affecting cost growth in acquisition programmes, including development strategy, schedule related factors, performance goals, management complexity and budget trends. Sometimes the length of a programme is associated with increased costs. The assertion is that longer programmes cost more, regardless of whether or not technical or programmatic problems occur. For instance, a longer programme may include product improvements that increase both design costs and unit production costs, hence markedly influencing cost-effectiveness analyses for the lifetime of systems.

Some analyses show that the dominant cause of cost growth are decisions involving quantity variations, requirements growth and schedule changes. Cost growth in major systems programmes also results from errors in estimation and scheduling, financial matters and miscellaneous sources.

A few basic steps may help prevent the occurrence of undesirable cost growth:

1. early, accurate cost estimates;

2. judiciousness in starting new programmes;

3. a focus on requirements.

The lifetime objective of System Effectiveness, in close correlation with Systems Life Cycle Cost, is to be taken into account since the very early stages of the life cycle, in which a larger degree of freedom is allowed in the implementation of system requirements. From a quantitative point of view, the effectiveness of a generic system is defined as a function of system performance and mission profile. As will be examined later in more detail, System Effectiveness is a measure of the ability of a system to achieve a set of specific mission requirements, namely to operate (in probabilistic terms of duration, repetition and efficacy) during a specified operational mission.

The subject of Life Cycle Cost, however, is also remarkable for a wider range of engineering disciplines, for example those of interest to the construction industry. In the case of buildings, Life Cycle Cost is typically part of Whole Life Cost (WLC), which also includes non-construction costs (land cost, financial costs, rental costs, management costs, taxes) and costs of externalities.

Another noteworthy area of application is railway engineering, where a number of current studies are based on life cycle cost-effectiveness evaluations.

It can be, therefore, concluded that the scope of cost-effectiveness encompasses almost the totality of complex engineering projects.

Book Overview

In the first part of this book, basic concepts of systems life cycle and related economic aspects are reviewed for an introductory, albeit expectantly comprehensive, discussion of Systems Life Cycle Cost analysis and estimation.

The second part emphasizes a wide range of applications to give the reader more insight into the basic concepts that were discussed preliminarily.

Appendices of this book address specific mathematical elaborations of the concepts of Learning Curves in Life Cycle Cost evaluation and considerations on System Effectiveness and Life Cycle Cost.

The book is intended for anyone concerned with system life cycle cost effectiveness, in the professional, government, industrial or academic environment. It will be of specific interest to engineers and managers involved in acquisition programmes.

Acknowledgements

This book could have never been written without the essential support originating from personal contacts and frequent meetings with valuable cost experts to whom I am deeply indebted: first of all, Marcel Smit, from TNO, The Netherlands, who acted as a valuable chairman in a number of NATO cost specialist working groups where I was the Italian representative; a huge number of former colleagues in Europe, USA and Canada; and, last but not least, in UK, Arthur Griffiths who, during his tenure as Chairman of the Society of Cost Analysis and Forecasting, kept me constantly aware of the advancement of SCAF activities.

As regards the life cycle cost-effectiveness of software-intensive systems, I certainly will not forget to mention the beneficial contribution deriving from my personal correspondence with such prominent experts as Ricardo Valerdi and especially Capers Jones.

Massimo Pica, Gen. (ret.)
Roma, Italy
January 2014

About the Author

Massimo Pica (massimo.pica@libero.it – mpica1949@alice.it) is a registered engineer in Rome, Italy.

After graduating in Chemical Engineering from Sapienza University in Rome, he spent more than 30 years in the Corps of Professional Engineers of the Italian Army and retired in 2009 as a one-star General.

He holds professional qualifications in Systems Engineering and Cost Management. His skills and expertise cover training and specialist writing on cost engineering and engineering economy; cost management, planning, reporting and control; project estimation and control; Earned Value Management; Cost Benefit Analysis.

He participated in national, international and NATO acquisition programmes and working groups specializing in Life Cycle Cost Management.

He is one of the authors of the two NATO Publications *RTO TR-SAS-054 – Methods and Models for Life Cycle Costing* and *RTO TR-SAS-069 – Code of Practice for Life Cycle Costing*. He is also a contributor to the NATO Publications *ALCCP-1 – NATO Guidance on Life Cycle Costs* and *RTO TR-SAS-076 – NATO Independent Cost Estimating and the Role of Life Cycle Cost Analysis in Managing the Defence Enterprise* as well as to the updated Italian version of the INCOSE *Systems Engineering Handbook*.

His current affiliations include the Italian Total Cost Management Association (AICE, a member of ICEC), the Italian Project Management Institute (ISIPM), the Italian Chemical Engineering Association (AIDIC), the European Committee of Construction Economists (CEEC) and the International Cost Estimating and Analysis Association (ICEAA).

PART ONE
Basic Concepts

Systems Design and the Characterization of Systems Requirements

'Seek first to understand. Then to be understood' (S.R. Covey)

Systems Engineering, Human Systems Integration and Life Cycle Cost

The devil is in the cost details. At least, this is the case for systems users around the world who face the herculean task of procuring, deploying and maintaining systems, equipment and material in a reliable condition. If, generically speaking, we refer to a 'system' as every type – however complex – of asset released as a result of a design effort, system procurement processes are influenced, in most cases, not only by the initial purchasing cost of a system, but particularly by all costs arising before and after the system is delivered for operational use. This would also include a specific retirement stage at the end of the system life cycle. The total amount of these costs, for a single system, is referenced in this book as *Life Cycle Cost* (LCC).

Designing a system, component or process to meet desired needs is a decision-making process (usually iterative) in which the basic sciences, mathematics and the engineering sciences are applied to convert resources optimally to meet these stated needs.

Typical users expectations are for systems that comply with operational needs and are reliable and competitive from the point of view of costs (that is, LCC) throughout the system life cycle. Life Cycle Cost is (or, indeed, *should be*) the dominating economic element in the selection of affordable systems to be procured and delivered: in fact, this sort of decision is influenced not only by the initial unit acquisition cost but, more significantly, by all subsequent unit costs, including retirement. Therefore in principle – albeit ideally – all different parties empowered in the management of the whole life cycle of systems should be involved from the beginning in decisions affecting systems Life Cycle Cost.

While systems are primarily designed to accomplish specified functions and operations, Systems Engineering principles (in the broadest context of the terminology) are commonly applied to certain advanced technology areas such as aerospace, electronics, ICT, but a system can be nevertheless identified as the product of any generic, industrial or civil, engineering effort intended to implement more or less complex functions (namely, ranging from a process plant to a residential area).

In summary, one of the key objectives of Systems Engineering is to realize systems that can perform their mission as cost-effectively as possible, taking into consideration the whole performance – cost – schedule – risk targets over the system life cycle. The *Systems Engineering Handbook* of the INCOSE (*International Council on Systems Engineering*) notes that '*As both complexity and change continue to escalate in our products, services, and society, reducing the risk associated with new systems or modifications to complex systems continues to be a primary goal of the systems engineer*'; and subsequently: '*New systems are designed, developed, manufactured, and verified over the span of many years, as in the case of a new automobile, or nearly two decades, as in the case of a submarine. Over such lengths of time, decisions made at the outset may have substantial, long-term effects that are frequently difficult to analyze*'.

An understanding of the extent of information affecting systems design is also important for a cost-effective management of the Systems Engineering effort, in accordance with the following basic elements:

- Comprehensive knowledge of system life cycle objectives.

- Appraisal of System Requirements.

- System definition.

- System implementation and integration.

- System assessment.

The operational need and/or commercial opportunity is expected to be initially rather unclear, so that the Systems Engineering effort, taking also into account any specific contractual, financial or technical constraints, should be initiated by a thorough exploration of how operational needs or commercial opportunities are perceived by all interested parties, while resolving in a timely fashion any conflicting judgements or, possibly, preventing their unwanted occurrence.

Systems Engineering is applied iteratively in order to release to users systems satisfying operational needs or commercial opportunities. On the basis of an appropriate understanding of operational requirements, Systems Engineering supports the specification, design, development and integration of systems of interest in agreement with a 'customer-centric' perspective. The compliance of the system to the requirements will be finally assessed as the system is developed.

Systems Engineering is also focused on the reconciliation between two different positions, namely those of the customer and of the designer/manufacturer. The customer will look at system functions and system performance to achieve operational goals and at system operational availability, usability, safety and maintainability to optimize life cycle expenditures. The designer/manufacturer will, in turn, look at meeting commercial needs, at efficient producibility, at business growth potential and reputation.

Long-term system success and user satisfaction rely deeply upon demonstrated effectiveness of the total system inclusive of personnel. In all systems, failure to address long-term, life cycle issues can result in failure to accomplish the intended purpose/mission, a poor design, unnecessary manpower burden, increased incidence of human errors, excessive Life Cycle Costs and, in some cases, negative impacts to the environment and public health and safety. Moreover, economic penalties may include loss of customer confidence, reduced market share and occurrence of product liability. Without this total system approach, the system as an enterprise solution will not meet optimal total performance and/or Life Cycle Cost objectives.

On the other hand, system design is not exclusively based on engineering practices. Development of creativity, ability to approach open issues and other more personal skills are useful in safeguarding conformity to practical constraints such as economic factors, safety, reliability, aesthetics, ethics and social impact.

The widespread application of Human Systems Integration (HSI) to system life cycle is intended to optimize total system performance (that is, human, hardware and software), while accommodating the characteristics of the personnel that will operate, maintain and support the system, including appropriate support measures to reduce costs across the entire system life cycle.

Human Systems Integration helps designers focus on long-term costs since a major percentage of Life Cycle Cost is related directly to human performance. It is critical to include HSI early in system acquisition (specifically, in the timeframe of capabilities requirements generation) and continuously through the acquisition process to realize the greatest benefit to the final system solution and substantial LCC reductions.

HSI implementation emphasizes the role of human contribution to system cost effectiveness. In addition, HSI is one of the essential components of engineering practice for system acquisition, providing technical and management support to the acquisition process itself. Human considerations that need to be addressed in system acquisition should specify the number and type of personnel in the various occupational areas required and potentially available to train, operate, maintain and support the deployed system. The personnel community promotes pursuit of engineering designs that optimize the cost-effective use of human resources, keeping their costs at affordable levels. Determination of required personnel positions should recognize the developing burdens on humans (for example, in terms of cognitive, physical and physiological characteristics) and consider how technology can affect individuals integrated into a system.

Concurrent assessment of HSI issues across all the domains and against mission performance is needed prior to undertaking formal programmatic commitments. This approach alleviates the perspective of unintentional, negative consequences, including higher technical risks and ensuing costs.

HSI requirements should be effectively coordinated with other system requirements and should consider any constraints or capability gaps. The human (and, consequently, ergonomic) aspects identified in the requirements should address the capabilities and limitations of all personnel interacting with or within the system. HSI requirements should be reviewed, refined and modified as programme documents, system requirements and specifications are updated. If these actions are undertaken from the beginning, regularly and carefully, then this will positively contribute to the acknowledgement of the risks and costs associated with programme decisions. HSI should be part of the initial life cycle strategy and LCC and life cycle sustainment documents.

Systems designers and HSI specialists should be prepared to present accurate, integrated cost data whenever possible to demonstrate reduced Life Cycle Costs, thereby justifying trade-off decisions that may influence acquisition costs as a result of more accurate design.

Human Factors (HFs) are a direct application of ergonomics, which is the scientific study of human work. HFs have been defined by the International Ergonomics Association (IEA) as '*the scientific disciplines concerned with the understanding of the interactions among human and other elements of a system and the profession that applies theory, principles, data and methods to design in order to optimize well-being and overall system performance*'. HFs analyze systems with a human-based approach, looking at individual systems from the users perspective, designing interactions with a system in compliance with operator profiles. Operator interaction with the system is performed through the utilization of a Human Machine Interface (HMI) mechanism, by inserting information to setup system capabilities and checking operational results to monitor the system behaviour. Interaction means that the operator is an active entity of the system.

HF engineering (that is the set of activities concerning HFs related matters identified through Systems Engineering processes) is applicable to all human-operated equipment and systems, however simple they might be.

Definition of System Requirements

The system design shall offer facilities to provide the relevant information to the right operators. The pursuit of this key aspect should always drive the system design. Failure to recognize and address likely human performance characteristics often leads to systems that do not meet their requirements or that experience unwanted breakdowns or cost growth.

Better requirements, which are an essential part of the technical baseline of a system acquisition programme, provide a primary opportunity for improving the outcomes of the system life cycle in the usual terms of cost, schedule and product quality.

In the past, requirements problems were typically considered as the single biggest contributor to cost overruns, schedule slippages and loss of capability in systems and software projects. Current reports in the UK only partially agree with this statement and are attributing the biggest contributor to the impacts from schedule delay caused by indifferent or poor management decision making. This sort of debate is still continuing in light of financial budget cuts and this, in itself, has caused amendments to the requirements (bit of a causal loop).

Table 1.1 is a classification of typical requirements.

Table 1.1   Classification of typical requirements

TYPE OF REQUIREMENT	CRITERION
State/Mode	States the required states and/or modes of the system, or the required transition between one state and another state, between one mode and another mode, between mode in one state to mode in another state (A 'state' is a condition of something. A 'mode' is a group of functionality related to purpose).
Functional	States what the item is to do.
Performance	For a given function, states *how well* that function is to be accomplished by the item.
External Interface	States the required characteristics at a localized point, or region, of connection of the system to the outside world.
Environmental	Limits the effect that the external enveloping environment (natural or induced) is to have on the item and the effect that the system is to have on the external enveloping environment.
Resource	Limits the usage or consumption of an externally provided resource by the system.
Physical	States the required *physical characteristics* (properties of matter) of the system as a *whole* (for example: mass, size, volume)
Other Quality	States any other required quality of the item that is not one of the above types, nor is a design requirement.
Design	Directs the design (internal components of the system), by inclusion ('*build it internally this way*') or exclusion ('*do not build it internally this way*')

In this context, requirements and resulting operational concepts will be translated into preliminary design documents, models, and prototypes, accompanied by relevant life cycle schedule elements and by initial cost estimates.

System functions need to be specifically identified. The system will be required to perform certain operations and support functions; consideration will be properly given to how well the system is required to perform each function, to the conditions under which the system is to begin performing that function, is to be capable of performing that function and is to finish performing that function. Conditions for the performance of required functions may include a reference to states and required modes of operation of the system.

The functional boundary of the system is expressed in terms of the expected external behaviour and properties. The required interactions between the system and its environment are analyzed and described in terms of interface constraints such as mechanical, electrical, thermal, dimensional, and procedural. This establishes the expected system behaviour, expressed in quantitative terms, at its boundary.

Subsequently, existing and/or planned support resources are established to identify and develop hardware/software design criteria and support structure design criteria for the proposed system, optimizing the utilization of those resources.

The next step in this process is the recognition of technologies applicable to the new design to improve supportability, decrease costs, and/or achieve a better balance between supportability and costs without any loss in performance. This effort is focused on the drivers identified as the first targets for improvement and is based on the analysis of the available technologies to determine their applicability to the new system. In addition, risks involved in the application of any new technology to the new design are investigated.

Non-functional requirements are addressed afterwards. These requirements pose constraints on the system design, specifically in the areas of reliability, maintainability, operability, safety, security, engineering standards, environment and support.

System requirements specifications, in the following step, define what the system should do to meet its capability objectives as dictated by the user community. A functional model of the system should be constructed by recognizing and decomposing the functions needed to achieve the required capabilities. System requirements should be baselined, documented and maintained under configuration control over the system life cycle, along with the associated rationale, assumptions and decisions.

Formal *System Requirements Reviews* (SRR) may be planned to analyze the integrity of system requirements, at a point in time when a significant portion of the system functional requirements has been established. Each statement of system requirements is examined to establish that it is necessary, implementation independent (that is, specifying *'what'* is to be done at a certain level, not *'how'* it is to be done at that level), clear, concise, traceable and verifiable. Deficiencies, conflicts and weaknesses are identified and resolved within the complete set of system requirements. These are then investigated to ensure that they are complete, consistent, achievable – given current technologies or awareness of technological improvements – and expressed at an appropriate level of detail. System requirements should essentially be a necessary and sufficient response to capability needs and a necessary and sufficient input to system design efforts, where system requirements will be allocated to the elements of system architecture.

Traceability between system requirements and capability needs should be demonstrated so that all achievable capability needs are met by one or more system requirements and all system requirements meet or contribute to meeting at least one capability need. System requirements are held in a suitable information database enabling traceability to capability needs and system architectural design.

2

The Life Cycle of Systems

In order to evaluate the Life Cycle Cost of a given system, a basic knowledge of the evolution of the life cycle schedule, and of the procedures involved in the life cycle management, is required. ISO/IEC 15288, '*Systems and software engineering – System life cycle processes*', describes the stages and processes included in the life cycle of systems. The accompanying ISO/IEC 12207, '*Systems and software engineering – Software life cycle processes*' should be considered as an additional reference for system software.

One of the basic decisions to be made is to choose between the design of a new system (that is, the *make* option) and the purchase of a system already delivered and available on the market (the *buy* option). In the first of the two instances, Life Cycle Cost studies may be required, so that the LCC can be quantitatively determined, for example, for the purpose of comparing alternative solutions or different economic options, thereby aiming at the best choice between the different alternatives.

In many cases, LCC studies have to be reiterated along the life cycle, for example to support modifications of user requirements or configuration change proposals.

According to ISO/IEC 15288, the life cycle of a generic system is composed of the following stages in a (hypothetical) sequential arrangement:

- Concept Stage

- Development Stage

- Production Stage

- Utilization Stage and Support Stage (which run simultaneously and may be grouped together as In-Service Stage)

- Retirement Stage

The decision between the two aforementioned options ('*make or buy*'), as pointed out in the *NATO Guidance on Life Cycle Costing* (see Bibliography), can take place, in the most suitable manner, at the completion of the Concept Stage, when system requirements become stabilized.

An alternative arrangement of the system life cycle can be identified as evolutionary acquisition. In this case, an acquisition programme evolves to its ultimate capabilities on the basis of mature technologies and available resources. Evolutionary acquisition is supported by incremental development and spiral development. In incremental development, a desired capability is established at the beginning of the programme and is met over time by developing several increments (or builds), each dependent on available mature technology. In spiral development, a desired capability is identified but the end-state requirements are not yet known.

Concept Stage

The Concept Stage (frequently following a preliminary exploratory technology research stage) is launched as a result of the decision to proceed with a system solution to implement an identified capability need and ends with the requirements specification for this system solution. The purpose is to evaluate the needs, potential risks and cost benefit of a proposed system or a major upgrade of an existing system prior to any commitment of resources. One or more alternative solutions to meet the identified need or concept are devised through analysis, feasibility evaluations, estimations (such as cost, schedule, market intelligence and logistics), trade-off studies and experimental or prototype development and demonstration.

The commencement of the Concept Stage is, consequently, based on the identification of a system need and on the decision in favour of an acquisition programme for the release of a system complying with the recognized capability requirement or, if more appropriate, to modify an existing system. At least two alternative solutions will be derived from the initial need or idea and examined in detail through an analysis process.

Feasibility studies are intended to investigate possible options on the basis of technical, economic and operational assessments in compliance with the requirements specified by the final user for the system life cycle management, aiming at an optimal solution in all its respects.

The basic purpose of these preliminary elements is to establish the worthiness of proceeding further into the system design and, specifically, of entering the Development Stage. Of course, if no sufficient conditions are available to keep the acquisition programme ongoing, it will have to be, regretfully but quite rightfully, abandoned.

Furthermore, experience has indicated that appropriate methodologies, technologies, tools and human resources are required in order to support life cycle activities, to be scheduled on the basis of an *affordability* assessment (that is, demonstration of cost-effective system capabilities). Affordability is the degree to which funding requirements for an acquisition programme fit within the customer's overall budget. Affordability analysis ensures that the programme has an adequate budget for its planned resources; whether an acquisition programme is affordable depends enormously on the quality of its cost estimate.

Primary intentions of the Concept Stage are to explore new commercial opportunities and to define system requirements and implementation criteria for the solutions that will have been recognized as feasible.

Development Stage

The purpose of the Development Stage is to progress the system configuration design in compliance with procurement requirements and in accordance with established practices for producibility, testability, usability, supportability and safe disposal.

The Development Stage begins with the definition of adequate details for a technical formulation of system requirements and of hypothetical solutions for requirements implementation, taking into account prospective users' needs.

In this context, prototype construction can take place, along with the specification of hardware and software elements and interfaces for integration and required evaluation tests. Additionally, consideration is given to requirements for production, training and support equipment.

Relevant parties (*stakeholders*) will also have to contribute to the assessment of all design enablers for the smooth evolution of the system life cycle, up to and including the final Retirement Stage. The outcome will be a preliminary system configuration, as well as technical documentation and an estimate of future costs. Previous life cycle activities will also result in the availability of various methodologies, techniques, tools and human resources required to undertake all efforts connected to analyses, modelling and simulation, prototyping, design, integration, testing and processing of technical documentation.

Production Stage

The purpose of the Production Stage is to manufacture/fabricate system components, execute system tests and prepare the tools required for production support.

The Production Stage can include specific integration, assembly and test processes, on a case-by-case basis. As a follow-up of previous planning efforts, there is a possibility that system configuration needs redesigns or upgrades, whenever stakeholders dictate improvements in the cost-effectiveness area.

Facilities, plants, equipment, operational procedures and skilled human resources will have to be available to start the production. They will be properly accounted for in the Life Cycle Cost of the system.

In Service – Utilization Stage

The purpose of the Utilization Stage is to operate system elements in accordance with the established operational procedures, in an appropriate and effective way.

The Utilization Stage begins with the delivery and start-up of the system and its components. System performance is closely monitored and anomalies, deficiencies and failures are identified, classified and reported. There are several remedies to solve identified problems: the typical choice is between no action, execution of maintenance activities, execution of temporary or permanent modifications (in accordance with specific Configuration Management practices and requirements).

The pre-requisite is the availability of appropriate facilities, equipment, skilled personnel, instruction manuals, operational procedures to enable an effective conduct of the Utilization Stage, until the system reaches the Retirement Stage.

In Service – Support Stage

The purpose of the Support Stage, which is concurrent with the Utilization Stage, is to ensure that the system can be correctly operated by means of appropriate logistics, maintenance and support services.

The Support Stage begins with the implementation of activities and means required to support system operation, in accordance with typical plans, for example an Integrated Support Plan (ISP) which should have been initially drafted during the Concept Stage, incorporating all specific plans such as a Reliability & Maintainability Plan.

Retirement Stage

The Retirement Stage includes system disposal (total or partial) whenever its operation is no longer required. This typically occurs if a new system is available as a replacement, if the system becomes irreversibly unreliable, or if cost-effectiveness requirements are not met anymore.

Care should be taken, on one side, to possibly recover (recycle) all reusable system elements (in order also to take advantage of their salvage value) and, on the other hand, to preserve all useful system information and all lessons learned during system lifetime, for possible future benefits and profitability.

Work Breakdown Structure

Every acquisition programme is based on a Work Breakdown Structure (WBS), which states in detail the work required to accomplish the objectives of the programme.

Specifically, a typical WBS derives from programme requirements and facilitates identification of resources and techniques for carrying out cost estimates for the programme. A WBS also offers a clear representation of what is to be done and how it is to be done.

The WBS is set up when the programme is established and further details are added subsequently as more information becomes available about the programme.

A WBS decomposes the end product of a programme into successive levels; its hierarchical structure shows how elements relate to one another as well as to higher level elements.

The number of levels for a WBS is different for different programmes and is affected by the specific complexity and risks of the programme. Work Breakdown Structures should be expanded to a level of detail that is adequate for planning and successfully managing the full scope of work of the programme. As a minimum, a WBS should include three levels. The first level (usually level 0) represents the programme in its entirety and therefore contains only one element: the name of the programme; the subsequent level 1 contains the major programme segments; the level 2 underneath contains lower level programme elements or subsystems for each segment. Further downwards, an empirical rule ('*5 per cent rule*') suggests that Work Packages placed at lower WBS levels should be, in turn, composed of Work Elements whose respective value should not be higher than 5 per cent of the overall value of the acquisition programme represented by the WBS.

A WBS is an essential management tool for an acquisition programme because it provides a basic context for a range of correlated activities like cost estimation, schedule development, resource planning, and risk management. The top-down, hierarchical nature of the WBS ensures nothing is missed in the programme planning process.

Tracking cost and schedule of acquisition programmes on the basis of a WBS allows programme managers to identify with a greater accuracy which elements are causing cost or schedule overruns and to mitigate the root cause of these overruns more effectively.

Failing to include the complete effort for all deliverables can lead to schedule delays and subsequent cost increases.

An initial WBS should be developed at an early stage of the programme to provide for a conceptual idea of programme size and scope. The WBS should mature as the programme evolves.

Consequently, as requirements are better defined and the statement of work is updated, the WBS will include more elements. At the same time, the greater definition of the schedule will give more insight into the programme cost, schedule and technical details.

It is essential that each WBS be accompanied by a *dictionary* of WBS elements and their hierarchical relationships. A WBS dictionary is simply a narrative description of the work to be performed in each WBS element. Like the WBS, its dictionary should be updated when changes occur.

Cost Breakdown Structure

While the Work Breakdown Structure (WBS) depicts specific elements of the system acquisition programme, thereby defining the scope of the programme, the Cost Breakdown Structure (CBS) serves the purpose of identifying all functions and tasks of future system life cycle, down to the proper decomposition level that best ensures the required cost element visibility, so that an estimated cost can be associated to each element; this will enable a timely refinement of LCC analysis process. A *CBS Dictionary* provides a summary description of cost categories included in the CBS and of formulae correlating cost elements at different CBS levels.

A CBS can positively facilitate the cost estimation process if it complies with a number of requirements, including the following:

- Simplicity of representation, utilization and update;

- Completeness of identification of relevant cost elements;

- Comparability with elements considered in cost estimation;

- Unambiguity of cost element definition;

- Flexibility of adaptation to peculiar programme characteristics across the entire life cycle.

Cost estimation is carried out for the different CBS categories, in each year of the system life. Cost estimates should account, to the most practicable extent, for inflation effects and for all other aspects that can contribute to cost variations, both positive and negative (for example, cost reductions can be induced by learning effects in series productions, as will be examined in Appendix 1 of this book). Cost estimates can also be originated from historical data or applicable quotations, in addition to usual estimating procedures.

3

Economic Principles and Applications of Life Cycle Cost Concepts, Life Cycle Cost, System Effectiveness and Figures of Merit

Present Value Analysis

This is a financial technique (also called discounting) used to compare costs and benefits occurring in various moments of a system life cycle, and specifically in each of the stages included in it.

For comparative purposes, all the expenses occurring in future periods should be referred to the same initial point in time of the entire period, taking into account an appropriate interest rate, which is a function of the period duration. These correction factors give the present value of £1 (or of a different currency) spent in each year: therefore, by discounting, different cash flows, corresponding to different periods, are transformed in equivalent values taking into account time related variations.

Net Present Value (NPV)

The present value of a series of payments is defined as the sum of payments made in an entire period (for example, the duration of an acquisition programme) discounted at a given interest rate.

Let us now consider the elements determining the present value.

Base year is the year to which all costs are referred. Usually this will be the first year of the period in which payments for the acquisition programme take place.

Period of analysis is usually the period ranging from the beginning of the acquisition programme to the completion of system mission. In most cases, this period denotes the system economic life, that is the period in which the benefits from system acquisition are expected to accrue; these benefits, eventually, are controlled by the physical duration of the system, which cannot be utilized further if the appropriate mission achievement is irreversibly prevented by deterioration or similar occurrence. Additionally, the economic life of a system can be constrained by the progress of technology: sooner or later, the system may become irrevocably obsolete, in accordance with the concept of technical life. In general, the economic life of a system is, therefore, referred to the period in which a specified mission or function is required and supported.

Having defined a base year and a period of analysis, the present value can be calculated on the basis of the known duration of payments required to deliver the system.

Subsequently:

- An appropriate discounting factor is selected for the period of payments and for each individual year of this period.

- Each annual cost is multiplied by the respective discounting factor.

- All discounted annual costs are summed up to obtain the total present value of costs. A similar procedure is followed for quantifiable benefits (that can be accounted for as incomes); the difference between the total present value of benefits and the total present value of costs is the Net Present Value (NPV).

An example of application of NPV to calculate the value of the optimum economic life of a generic system is provided in Appendix 2.

Constant Money and Current Money

Correlation of the following enables the financial analysis to be carried out correctly: i (interest rate or discounting rate inclusive of inflation), i' (interest rate neglecting the inflation) and f (annual inflation rate).

Using current money, as shown by Thuesen and Fabrycky (see Bibliography), the corresponding constant money (base year, $t = 0$) can be calculated by dividing the current money amount by the factor $(1 + i)^n$, n being the number of years after the initial year:

$$P = F \, \frac{1}{(1+i)^n}$$

In alternative, current money can be transformed into constant money and the equivalent value of that amount in constant money can be found in $t = 0$:

$$F' = F \, \frac{1}{(1+f)^n}$$

$$P = F' \, \frac{1}{(1+i')^n} = F \, \frac{1}{(1+f)^n} \, \frac{1}{(1+i')^n}$$

Since the values of P must be equal in the base year, the previous calculations yield:

$$F \, \frac{1}{(1+i')^n} = F \, \frac{1}{(1+f)^n} \, \frac{1}{(1+i')^n}$$

$$(1+i)^n = (1+f)^n (1+i')^n$$

$$1 + i = (1+f)(1+i')$$

$$i = (1+f)(1+i') - 1$$

$$i' = \frac{1+i}{1+f} - 1$$

We can proceed further to arrive at a representative expression for the Life Cycle Cost.

LCC is to be considered, as it actually is, composed by a certain number of cost elements (C_{mn}) characterized by a double subscript: m (indicating the cost element category, a whole number ranging between 1 and M) and n (indicating the year corresponding to the generic cost element, variable between 1 and N).

Since the cost values C_{mn} are future values, they can be discounted using the previous relationships. In particular, from

$$\frac{1}{(1+i')^n} = \left[\frac{1+f}{1+i}\right]^n$$

we finally obtain the following Life Cycle Cost formula:

$$LCC = \sum_{n=1}^{N} \left\{ \left[\frac{1+f}{1+i}\right]^n * \sum_{m=1}^{M} C_{mn} \right\}$$

Equivalent Annual Costs

The annual value gives an indication of costs expressed as equivalent payments made on an annual basis. The equivalent annual cost of a system can be simply evaluated by considering a sequence of n annual payments of equal value. If A is the annual payment, we have:

$$A = P \left[\frac{i\,(1+i)^n}{(1+i)^n - 1}\right]$$

In general, the constant annual value A is only part of the overall cash flow. In addition, this may include a uniform variation G (positive or negative) between a certain year and the subsequent year. Therefore, if A_1 is the first annual payment, the equivalent annual cost will be given by the following expression:

$$A = A_1 + G \left[\frac{1}{i} - \frac{n}{(1+i)^n - 1}\right]$$

If, instead, the annual increase occurs with a uniform percentage g between a certain year and the subsequent year, the following expression gives the present value P of a series of annual payments with a constant per cent gradient:

$$P = \frac{F_1}{1+g} \left[\frac{(1+g')-1}{g'(1+g')^n} \right]$$

where:

$$g' = \frac{1+i}{1+g} - 1$$

and F_1 is the first annual payment in the cash flow series.

The Total System Economic Value and the Life Cycle Cost

Daily decisions required to manage the introduction of new systems or the modification of existing systems often take into consideration only those technical characteristics that are deemed significant with respect to the expected system performance. From the economic point of view, most attention is attributed to initial acquisition costs, while much lesser attention, in a number of cases, is paid to costs related to subsequent life cycle stages, namely Utilization Stage and Support Stage (in which the system is, respectively, operated and maintained). Actually, Utilization and Support costs often play a major role in the context of the Life Cycle Cost of systems; furthermore, they are markedly determined by decision-making processes taking place at the inception of system lifetime.

As will be discussed in detail later in this book, the purpose of system LCC estimation is to ensure that all costs are properly taken into account and that the resulting LCC value is the minimum reasonably possible. Initial Life Cycle Cost elements may be recognized, in the Concept Stage, during feasibility studies, whereas, at the other end, the Retirement Stage embodies the final set of life cycle cost elements. LCC estimates should completely include all cost elements, individually identified; preparation of these estimates involves the translation of all technical characteristics and design parameters of the system – along with schedule elements of interest – into economic values through the adoption of well-established cost estimation methodologies.

Technical characteristics are assessed iteratively in design reviews, until it is recognized that, at an adequate confidence level, cost estimates are satisfactorily representative of basic design requirements and user needs, so that the acquisition programme budget can be outlined. As already mentioned, a great deal of attention is needed to cost rationalization measures, first of all in the system acquisition, but especially after system deployment. This essentially means that all programme decisions required in the life cycle of an innovative system should properly address the issue of cost growth limitation in connection with the introduction of unproven technologies or with other system specific factors.

As illustrated in Figure 3.1, the total system value derives from an appropriate balance between economic factors (essentially connected to benefit/cost ratio) and design factors (related to system effectiveness) relevant to the system under consideration. A generic list of cost elements encompassed in LCC includes, at the beginning, the feasibility studies, the initial drafting of technical and support requirements, the system analyses and subsequently the detailed system design and development effort, the design, assembly and test of engineering models, along with the documentation costs.

A subsequent set of cost elements refers to the manufacture, assembly and test of system prototypes, to special tools and equipment required to produce

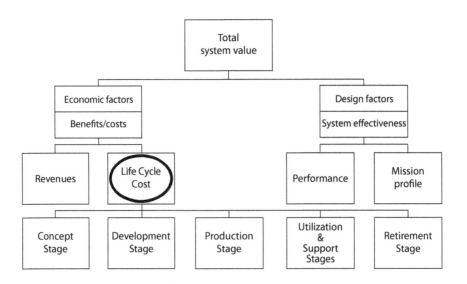

Figure 3.1   Total system value

the system and to the procurement of initial spares for system maintenance (including the necessary documentation).

It is to be noted that the costs incurred from the beginning of life cycle up to the completion of production should, clearly, be correlated with the entire quantity of systems produced. Therefore, the average unit acquisition cost (which will be hereafter denoted by the acronym LCCA) for each system will be calculated by dividing the total acquisition cost by the number of manufactured systems.

After the system is delivered, the user will incur its utilization and support costs, including: personnel, procurement of spares, maintenance management, test and support equipment, transportation and handling, facilities, software, modifications and technical data. At the end of its life cycle, the system is retired (especially because of its obsolescence or irreversible deterioration) and the user will incur system retirement cost. All these cost categories included in LCC should be, similarly, correlated with the quantity of systems for the purpose of (unit) LCC calculation on a homogeneous basis.

In the professional literature, one of the earliest complete treatments of Life Cycle Cost is found in the book '*Design and Manage to Life Cycle Cost*' by B.S. Blanchard (see Bibliography). B.S. Blanchard, Professor Emeritus at Virginia Institute of Technology, in this best-selling book, albeit written more than 30 years ago, and in a number of further publications captured the iceberg picture (Figure 3.2) to represent the contrast between the acquisition costs (relatively well known, hence placed above the water line) and the ownership and retirement costs (largely unknown, therefore represented below the water level).

Two main aspects conceptually significant for the life cycle of any system are emphasized by Blanchard, namely:

- The different '*visibility*' of Life Cycle Cost components (in accordance with the iceberg metaphor);

- the fact that it is at the early stages in an acquisition programme that the greatest gains can be realized in terms of the system Life Cycle Cost (however taking cautiously into account some downstream events often occurring during the life of the system, influencing the Life Cycle Cost itself, for example: life cycle schedule slips, changes in quantity of systems to be installed and/or in their operational conditions; significant improvement programmes).

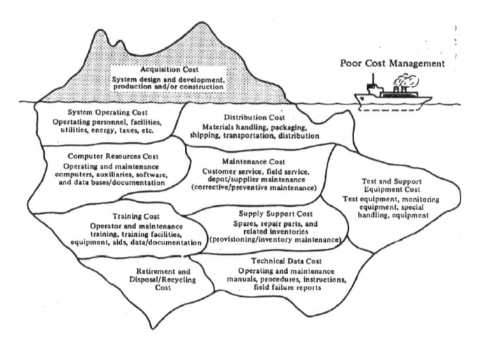

Figure 3.2   Cost visibility over a system life cycle ('cost iceberg')

System LCC is predominantly of interest to different parties which – as noted by Blanchard – contribute, for various reasons, to '*bringing a system into being*': the manufacturer, the purchaser and the final user.

Early initiatives on Life Cycle Costing took place in the Sixties, when the US Department of Defense inaugurated its utilization in the procurement of military equipment. LCC concept and its application criteria were first considered by the US Government specifically due to the fact that acquisition costs were found to be often largely less than utilization and support costs, which in certain cases reached as much as 75 per cent of total cost.

In the Seventies, applications of LCC concepts were extended to encompass preliminary decision-making processes in early design phases, in order to assess system configurations on the basis of requirements for lower utilization and maintenance costs, typically by rigorous management of preventive and corrective maintenance.

An international treatment of LCC can be found in the IEC standard 60300-3-3:2004 '*Dependability management Part 3-3: Application Guide – Life cycle costing'*. Other LCC standards and applicable literature are mentioned in the Bibliography section.

Figures of Merit

LCC estimation process offers a number of basic elements to support decisions not only during the early life cycle stages, but in all subsequent periods. Specific decisions are required to manage maintenance policies and to carry out trade-offs between different possible alternatives, until the system life comes to its projected (and maybe, to some extent, unpredicted) end.

The following relationship:

$$FOM = \frac{SE}{LCC}$$

introduces the helpful quantitative tool called '*Figures of Merit*' (FOM), by which any system to be procured can be characterized on the basis of calculated values of System Effectiveness (dimensionless) and Life Cycle Cost (in currency units).

From a quantitative point of view, the effectiveness of a generic system is defined as a function of system performance and mission profile. It has to be considered as a goal to be taken into account since the very early stages of the life cycle, in which a larger degree of freedom is allowed in the implementation of system requirements:

$$SE = A_0 * D_0 * C$$

where:

SE (System Effectiveness) is a measure of the ability of a system to achieve a set of specific mission requirements.

A_0 (Operational Availability) is a measure of the degree to which a system is in the operable and committable state at the start of the mission, when the mission is called for at an unknown (random) time.

D_0 (Operational Dependability) is a measure of the degree to which a system is operable and capable of performing its required function at any (random) time during a specified mission profile, given system availability at the start of the mission.

C (Capability) is a measure of the ability of an item to achieve mission objectives, given the conditions during the mission.

Figure 3.3 depicts a breakdown of System Effectiveness in its typical lower level components.

The first level components of System Effectiveness, Availability, Dependability and Capability, are therefore measures of system ability to operate (in probabilistic terms of duration, repetition and efficacy) during a specified operational mission. System Effectiveness may be regarded as a collective term used to describe the system availability performance and its design factors, namely reliability, maintainability and logistic support.

Figures of Merit are also dependent on Life Cycle Cost, so that LCC values, calculated for a range of solutions to be evaluated for their feasibility, will be correlated with the corresponding values of System Effectiveness.

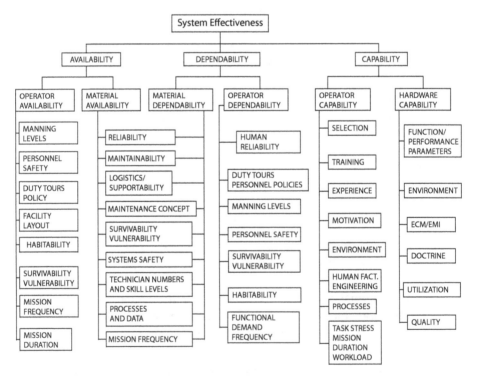

Figure 3.3   Components of System Effectiveness

For a given system, any increase of MTBF (mean time between consecutive failures) requires higher initial investment costs and higher production costs, due to the insertion of more reliable components. This is counterbalanced by lower costs for logistics (equipment and labour), including maintenance, both corrective and programmed.

Whenever a system becomes unavailable, its LCC can be significantly affected. Actually, failures or malfunctions require using alternative equipment or terminating a mission, both of which cause an increase in LCC. There is also an analytical correlation between the failure frequency at component level and the mean time to repair the system and restore its functionality (usually abbreviated as MTTR), which, in turn, influences the system downtime.

It becomes, therefore, necessary to optimize availability values with respect to Life Cycle Costs. LCC is optimized when the increase of acquisition costs due to reliability improvements is equal to the resulting decrease of operational and support costs: the point of minimum LCC (all other conditions remaining unchanged), corresponds to the optimum value of system reliability.

FOM is a Cost-Effectiveness parameter synthesizing the overall life-long system performance and its corresponding cost, referred to the whole system life cycle.

Acquisition, ownership and retirement costs should be estimated as soon as possible, so that responsible authorities can find an optimum balance between System Effectiveness factors and Life Cycle Cost.

4

Fundamentals of Life Cycle Cost Analysis

Life Cycle Cost Profile and Summary

By using the notion of Life Cycle Cost (LCC), the objective of cost-effectiveness for a given system is considered from a total system life cycle perspective. All decisions made on the system design and manufacture may affect its performance, safety, reliability, maintainability, and so on, consequently determining its price and ownership costs. By performing trade-off studies on LCC the system design can be optimized from the LCC viewpoint.

Comparing performance between different systems is not a comfortable job, but comparing Life Cycle Costs is likely to be essentially harder. It is therefore necessary to introduce many assumptions about the systems and in some situations, where realistic assumptions are hard to give, indications on the variations relative to different variables have to be given as a substitute.

A basis for all cost considerations is that the requirements express all needs of a system and of its components.

If we consider the requirements as constant and not subject to change, the objective is to design, build, operate and maintain a system that satisfies these requirements as inexpensively as possible, until this system is retired. The assumption that improved performance is not an option, to reduce requirements in order to save cost, may in some situations be wrong since the objective instead can be to realize a trade-off between effectiveness and cost. In such a situation system requirements are not considered as fixed.

The LCC estimate should include all cost elements, with their estimated costs, which are derived from a technical assessment of the system, as well as from schedule elements of interest; all of these are translated into economic values, using appropriate cost analysis techniques. Technical issues are iteratively re-examined in specific design reviews before reaching confidence concerning compliance of basic design requirements, capability requirements and fitness to operational scenarios, with respect to the assumptions taken into account in the cost estimates. This is when the budget for the system acquisition programme can be prepared.

In budgeting for the LCC, if all costs are expressed as *present values*, referred to a single initial point in time, for each year of system lifetime, an 'equivalence base' is created, so that LCC values can be estimated and compared for the possible range of different alternatives envisaged.

Of course, annual costs are subject to the variable incidence of inflation rates; this, in turn, influences the annual expenditure planning, based on the actual value year by year.

Subsequently, likely 'causes' of cost elements identified in the CBS will be determined. In each case, analysts will have to re-examine the CBS, the assumptions made to determine costs and the Cost Estimating Relationships (CERs) used in the analysis process.

At this moment, it will be necessary to confirm the soundness of results, taking into account input data and confidence level for the estimate. Therefore, a sensitivity analysis will be executed with reference to input parameters that are deemed most critical. These will be varied in suitable ranges and the LCC analysis process will be repeated to appraise the corresponding results: the essential purpose of sensitivity analysis is, in fact, to identify parameters that, even with a small variation of their value, lead to a large variation in resulting cost.

Subsequently, LCC analysis considers possible alternative solutions resulting from a feasibility study of system implementation.

Table 4.1 presents the results of LCC estimation for two possible system configurations, showing Present Values of high level CBS cost elements.

Table 4.1   LCC estimation for alternative system configurations

Cost categories	Configuration A		Configuration B	
	Cost k£	% LCC	Cost k£	% LCC
Concept, Development	70	7.8	53	4.2
o Management	9	1.0	9	0.7
o Design	46	5.1	29	2.3
o Test	12	1.4	12	1.0
o Technical documentation	3	0.3	3	0.2
Production	408	45.3	331	26.1
o Investment on facilities	45	5.1	43	3.4
o Manufacture	363	40.2	288	22.7
Utilization and Support	420	46.6	880	69.4
o Operations	38	4.2	39	3.1
o Maintenance	382	42.4	841	66.3
- personnel	211	23.4	407	32.1
- spares and repair parts	103	11.5	229	18.1
- test equipment	48	5.3	132	10.4
- transportation	14	1.6	52	4.1
- maintenance training	2	0.2	2	0.2
- facilities and ancillaries	1	0.1	1	0.1
- data management	3	0.4	18	1.4
Retirement	2	0.2	3	0.3
Life Cycle Cost	900	100	1,268	100

It is a primary purpose of Life Cycle Cost assessment to provide input to decisions occurring across the life cycle. LCC assessment is an essential pre-requisite for a number of life cycle aspects, including the following:

- Evaluation and comparison of alternative design approaches and technological solutions;

- Affordability estimates;

- Identification of cost drivers and cost-effective improvements;

- Evaluation and comparison of alternative strategies for system operation, test, maintenance;

- Evaluation of possible system life extensions;

- Allocation of available funds to design alternatives and system improvements;

- Multi-year financial planning.

A critical requirement of LCC analysis is to assess programme affordability by identifying relevant cost drivers as connected with specific elements of operational need (Key Performance Indicators/Parameters, Key User Requirements).

Furthermore, it is to be noted that, at the launch of a programme, the order of magnitude of future Utilization and Support costs can be only foreseen with a rough approximation. This introduces a significant uncertainty/risk factor in the assessment of total LCC, especially if comparable data cannot be derived from similar pre-existing programmes.

Retirement costs (which are also 'invisible' in the iceberg metaphor) may not always play a minor role; in certain cases, large expenditures are required by applicable legislations for disposal activities (for example, if a significant amount of nuclear components is part of the system under consideration).

General Criteria for Life Cycle Cost Analysis

LCC analysis is oriented towards long term economic factors in the life cycle of a generic system, rather than trying to save money in the short term by simply purchasing systems with lower initial acquisition costs. It allows an easier overall cost visibility and a straightforward evaluation of risks associated with decision-making processes connected with future costs until completion of system retirement.

LCC analysis is obviously significant both for systems entering their life cycle and for existing systems requiring an identification of most significant cost factors. The stepwise procedure typically followed in a LCC analysis is described in the subsequent sections.

If a LCC analysis is required, the initial approach to the analysis process should consider technical solutions for system configuration, on the basis of system operational requirements and support concept. Specifically, it is necessary to appraise the criticality of *Technical Performance Measures* (TPM) and to define the system in functional terms. This will give the possibility to evaluate system proposed architectures and to identify resources (hardware, software, personnel) required to achieve system operational purposes.

Since utilization and support costs are usually predominant, the aspects that mostly affect these costs have to be duly highlighted, including: geographical system location (and its impact on maintenance organization); daily and annual operational profile; effectiveness requirements in terms of MTBF, Corrective Maintenance Downtime, number of maintenance hours for every hour of operation, correlated with labour costs.

As anticipated in the introduction to Figures of Merit, each design option should be appraised bearing in mind its incidence on System Effectiveness and on overall costs that derive from selecting that option across the entire life cycle (that is, the System Life Cycle Cost).

LCC analysis takes into consideration various possible system design alternatives in economic terms by using a limited set of parameters, which nevertheless are correlated to all significant functional aspects of system supportability and elements and services for system maintenance.

In LCC analysis costs are estimated for all activities required in the system life cycle, in order to define and/or optimize technical and economic strategies associated with system acquisition, utilization and support. Accordingly, LCC analysis consists of an evaluation effort beginning in the preliminary design phase and extending through subsequent phases to gain confidence that the selected alternative is the best in terms of its Figure of Merit.

A Life Cycle Cost estimate provides a comprehensive and organized accounting of all resources and associated cost elements required to design, develop, produce, deploy and sustain a particular system. This requires identifying all cost elements that relate to the programme from initial concept all the way through operations, support and retirement. All past (unrecoverable or *sunk*) costs, present costs and future costs are encompassed in Life Cycle Cost estimation for every aspect of a system acquisition programme, irrespective of funding source.

Data Management for Life Cycle Cost Analysis

Data are the main source of every LCC analysis process. Data collection is an extensive practice, since several types of data have to be collected: for example, cost, schedule and technical data.

There are different options for data collection: historical programme data bases, engineering analysis, interviews, surveys.

Cost data management should be based on realistic schedule information; understanding the factors that affect programmes cost is essential for capturing the right data.

Data collection can be problematic when data definitions are inconsistent in historical acquisition programmes compared to a new programme. It is essential to recognize the content of historical data to ensure data reliability.

Cost data usually include amounts for labour, material and overheads, facilities capital cost of money and revenue associated with each activity.

Schedule or programme data provide factors that directly affect the total cost and, therefore, should be considered in developing a cost estimate: for example, lead-time schedules, start and duration of effort, delivery dates and other parameters that are relevant in specific cases.

Technical data identify the requirements for the system being estimated, based on physical and performance elements.

Since primary data for cost analysis are obtained from the original source, they should be used whenever possible. Instead, secondary data are originated in an indirect fashion: with respect to primary data, their overall quality is lower and less useful; cost estimators should pursue an understanding of how these secondary data were normalized, what the data represent, how recent they are, and whether they are complete.

If cost estimates are developed with data from past programmes, it is important to examine whether the historical data (very often deriving from legacy systems) apply to the new programme being estimated. Over time, modifications may have changed the past programme so that it is no longer similar to the new one.

Data Collection in Systems Life Cycle

Life cycle costing has been recognized as a data driven process. With regard to the time, effort and resources expended, collection of data is a major part of Life Cycle Cost studies.

It is imperative to remember that the quality and value of life cycle management and LCC analyses is very much correlated to the quality of the available data. Consequently, good data mean real value for a system acquisition programme. Conversely, real costs are associated with the collection and storage of data.

As a system progresses across its life cycle, the categories of data available develop in a number of ways. Since this, in turn, identifies the undertaking of data collection and the life cycle costing process in general, it is imperative to be aware of these developments.

Obviously, the knowledge about the end system is very little when an acquisition programme begins and only an identified capability gap or a general concept is available, whereas, when a system is in service, the system and its environment can be documented in good detail. Uncertainties, risks and opportunities decrease as the life cycle progresses and, therefore, the need for information is the highest at the earliest stages. In turn, this means that more time and more resources should be assigned to the data collection effort at the initial stages of the system life cycle.

The properties of the available data will change as well across the system life cycle. Initial data are likely to be in a more grouped form, since detailed information is not yet available.

Life cycle costing involves a wide multiplicity of data and these should be gathered from an even wider multiplicity of sources.

As already indicated, since initially the system is indefinite, the majority of data will come from outside the programme, originating from comparable systems and programmes. Therefore, in these early stages, comparable systems and programmes, as well as relevant data sources, should be identified.

Data from similar systems should then be adjusted on the basis of dissimilarities between systems with respect to performance, complexity, maturity of technology, and so on, greatly depending on the peculiarities of the individual programme, so that only specific methods can be applied. One of these methods is explained in Chapter 10 of the US Federal Aviation Administration's (FAA) publication *Life Cycle Cost Estimating Handbook* (see Bibliography). The following expression is used:

$$C_N = C_P * F_C * F_M * F_P$$

where the equivalent cost for the new system (C_N) is obtained from the non-recurring and first unit production cost of the previous system (or system component) (C_P), multiplied by a complexity factor ratio (F_C), a miniaturization factor ratio (F_M) and a productivity component ratio (F_P). The aforementioned US publication explains in detail the data requirements, the meaning of the terms and the procedure used to derive the cost for a new system from the cost of a selected previous system.

In addition, caution should be used to ensure that reference systems are in fact comparable to the system of interest. If the technology of the new system is completely different, if its operating profile is different and so on, data from existing systems may be irrelevant and the applicability of analogy methods would be excluded.

In the beginning, expert judgement or opinion may be the only available source of information on a system acquisition programme. Expert judgement, based on more or less well documented data and experiences, is largely impossible to validate, but it is useful if at all possible to get more than one opinion. This means that a more manual, creative, labour-intensive effort should be performed in the early stages of the life cycle.

Data Normalization

The aims of data normalization, that is the adjustment of cost data avoiding the effect of external influences, are the consistency of a given data set and the possibility to compare it with respect to other data used in the estimate.

Data collected from several sources are frequently in many different forms and have to be adjusted before being used for comparison purposes or as a basis for projecting future costs. For example, costs can be adjusted to a common year or to different inflation or discounting mechanisms or different variations in accounting standards, in accordance with the principles of economic equivalence.

As data consistency is improved, comparisons and projections are more valid and other data can be used to increase the number of data points.

Irrespective of how data are normalized, accurate, complete and detailed documentation of the normalization process is essential. This applies whenever normalization of primary data is done as part of the Life Cycle Cost estimating process or secondary data have been captured for use in Life Cycle Cost estimation. Serious mistakes can be made if data are not correctly understood and interpreted. It is therefore vital to thoroughly recognize data and to identify where data are coming from.

After the data have been collected, analyzed and normalized, they should be documented and stored for future use. Comprehensive documentation during the data collection process significantly improves quality and reduces subsequent effort in developing and documenting the estimate.

Previously documented cost estimates may provide useful data for a current estimate by eliminating the need to conduct statistical analyses that have already been conducted.

Properly documented estimates describe the data used to estimate each WBS element, and this information can be used as a good starting point for the new estimate. Moreover, relying on other programme estimates can be valuable in providing cross-checks for reasonableness.

For further insights on how cost data collection and subsequent normalization should be carried out, the (former) SCEA's (Society of Cost Estimating and Analysis) publication *Cost Estimating Body of Knowledge* (see Bibliography) can be consulted.

Other Relevant Factors in Life Cycle Cost Analysis

A number of factors affect LCC analysis processes and contribute to their complication. These factors need to be carefully explored.

In some cases, when addressing problems of selection between different alternatives, an opportunity cost is to be taken into account in LCC analysis. For example, if a system A has a certain estimated cost with a minimum risk and a challenger system B has an estimated cost 20 per cent lower than A, but with a higher risk, the alternative A could be selected, thereby considering the 20 per cent difference as the cost of not having pursued the opportunity of acquiring the system B, neglecting the risks.

LCC analyses are usually referred to constant money. This is due to difficulties in accurate predictions of inflation rates, continually affecting the time value of money. When the programme duration is short, a more reliable inflation rate can be forecast.

Taxes and subsidies can affect prices they refer to. Market prices inclusive of taxes, for LCC estimation purposes, should therefore (but also for other reasons) be considered on a case-by-case basis in the evaluation of investment alternatives, so that this evaluation can be correct.

As regards exchange rates, when they are required, there is a supply-and-demand mechanism that influences the market value of a currency. Fluctuations of exchange rates between different currencies should be taken into account as risk factors.

Discounting affects cash flows considered in investment studies. This is reflected both in the vast amount of relevant literature and also in the computer calculations of financial functions (for example, using spreadsheets or other appropriate programmes). Discounting is required whenever it is necessary to compare different investment alternatives on an equivalence basis, by determining the Net Present Value of various future cash flows.

Depreciation is an accounting technique for tax purposes, that accounts for the wearing out of assets by allocating their value over a certain period of time (depreciation is obviously different in concept from discounting).

In order for LCC analysis to produce results that can be efficiently and correctly utilized, the following procedure can be applied in a well-structured and documented fashion:

- Develop the LCC management plan;

- Select the LCC model ('make or buy', whether it is an in-house or commercial model);

- Apply LCC model;

- Document LCC analysis;

- Execute a final check of LCC analysis results;

- Update LCC analysis as appropriate.

Usually, this procedure takes place iteratively if it includes certain tasks providing for revisions and modifications of prior work. Assumptions considered in each step of the above procedure should be carefully documented to facilitate iterations as necessary and contribute to correct interpretations of analysis outcomes.

It should be remembered that LCC analysis is an interdisciplinary effort, requiring adequate familiarity with the principles governing the LCC concept applications (including cost elements and their generating causes and applicable financial guidelines) and a clear understanding of methods to assess margins of uncertainty/risk (whichever is applicable) associated to cost estimates. Depending on the area of application of LCC analysis, it is also important to translate information available on the system life cycle stages into cost elements.

To facilitate decisions, before entering into LCC analysis, the following aspects should be considered:

- Definition of analysis objectives with reference to expected results and to ensuing decisions;

- Definition of analysis scope, period of life cycle time to be accounted for, Utilization and Support scenario;

- Identification of all conditions, assumptions, limitations and constraints, for example minimum system performances, availability requirements or funding limitations, which are likely to circumscribe the range of acceptable options for selection;

- • Identification of alternative strategies;

- • Definition of an estimate of required resources, in order to ensure that results will be promptly obtainable to support decision making processes they are needed for.

As regards analysis objectives, they typically include:

- • LCC definition aimed at supporting plans, contractual procedures, budget development or similar necessities;

- • Evaluation of the extent to which LCC is affected by the diversity of options in executing the programme (for instance, in the design approach, in acquisition and support policies, in technology insertion);

- • Identification of major cost elements influencing LCC, for the purpose of optimizing design, development, acquisition and support tasks.

Execution of LCC analyses establishes a critical reference point in performing the entire subsequent procedure. Users concerned should be allowed to review analysis results to confirm that their needs are correctly interpreted and satisfactorily fulfilled. In this respect, a specific LCC Report, documenting LCC analysis results, could enable users to clearly understand analysis results and their implications, also taking into account limitations and uncertainties associated to results. Specifically, a summary of the LCC model is presented, including relevant assumptions, the LCC Breakdown Structure arrangement, the explanation of cost elements and of their evaluation and integration in the general Life Cycle Cost structure. Subsequently the results from the application of the LCC model are described, identifying major cost items and results of sensitivity analysis and of other analyses as appropriate.

5

Fundamentals of LCC Estimation

The Technical Baseline of Acquisition Programmes

Reliable LCC estimates result from a comprehensive approach to the acquisition programme they are prepared for, including the acquisition strategy, technical definition, characteristics, system design features and technologies relevant to system design. This information can be used to identify the technical and programme parameters that will affect the cost estimate. The amount of information collected has a direct incidence on the overall quality and flexibility of the estimate, whereas limited information would mean the need to make more assumptions and the consequential increase of the risk related to the estimate.

The technical baseline conveys in a single document a common definition of the programme, from which LCC estimates can be derived. Information in the technical baseline can sometimes facilitate the use of a particular estimating methodology.

In addition to providing a wide-ranging programme description, the technical baseline is used to benchmark Life Cycle Costs and identify specific technical and programme risks.

The technical baseline is expected to be updated in preparation for programme reviews, milestone decisions, and major programme changes. Reliable LCC estimates require that the technical baseline be regularly maintained.

Technical baselines of acquisition programmes evolve as new information becomes available. On the other hand, the technical baseline should provide the best available information at any point in time.

LCC estimation requires that technical baselines should be prepared for each alternative of system life cycle implementation; as the programme develops, the number of alternatives and, therefore, of technical baselines decreases.

The technical baseline should, primarily, include a description of the system mission and provide a notion of its complexity; a Work Breakdown Structure should be added to this description. The technical baseline should also describe key functional requirements and performance characteristics of the system, if appropriate with reference to an existing system which the new one is replacing.

Other significant elements are the acquisition strategy and schedule, the requirements concerning components and systems to be used for development and test, quantities to be produced, plans for system deployment/installation, utilization, support and retirement. Details on the practical use of these elements can be found, for example, in the *NASA Cost Estimating Handbook* (see Bibliography), which introduces the *Cost Analysis Data Requirement* (CADRe) as the basis for deriving a Life Cycle Cost estimate.

Whenever system requirements change, the technical baseline and LCC estimate should be updated.

The technical baseline should document the technical and programme assumptions on which the LCC estimate will be based, and should identify the level of risk associated with these assumptions.

Purpose, Scope and Schedule of LCC Estimates

The purpose of a cost estimate, and also its scope and level of detail, is influenced by its projected application.

The scope will be established on the basis of the time involved, the elements that have to be estimated, the personnel in charge of the cost estimates and the detail of the cost estimating effort.

The level of detail for the cost estimate as well as the amount of data to be gathered will be different depending on where the system is in the evolution of its life cycle.

Early Life Cycle Cost estimates will probably not entail extensive details. As the programme becomes better defined (for example, as the programme moves into system production), more details should be incorporated in subsequent estimates.

At an early stage, it may be preferable to perform the estimate at a relatively high system level to ensure that all the lower level elements are considered. The more detail is required, the more time and staff will be required for the estimate.

Ground Rules and Assumptions

Ground rules denote a common set of estimating guidelines aimed at minimizing conflicts in definitions. Assumptions denote a set of judgements hypothesized as correct in the absence of positive proof.

LCC estimates are generally based on limited information. Specialists use the term *epistemic uncertainty* to identify the effect of this lack of knowledge on the estimate, which is different in concept from the uncertainty deriving from the statistical nature of available information (that is, *statistical uncertainty*).

Because of the inherent unknowns, cost analysts should state a number of ground rules and assumptions providing a basis for the cost estimate that, in particular, identifies areas of potential risk.

When ground rules and assumptions have to be established, it is absolutely mandatory to define a realistic schedule. In establishing realistic schedules, the primary challenge is that frequently completion dates are dictated by external factors.

Overly optimistic assumptions could heavily influence the overall cost estimate, leading to likely cost overruns and to inaccurate estimates and budgets.

Methodologies for Life Cycle Cost estimation

LCC estimation process consists of a series of tasks that are mainly directed to the definition of system economic aspects, on the basis of the level of system complexity, of the cost estimation purposes, of the time when the estimation takes place and of the kind of cost data available for the estimation.

The arrangement of the Cost Breakdown Structure is directly affected by the system nature and complexity. The cost estimation purposes and the time when the estimation takes place, inside the system life cycle, are related to the deepest level of detail of cost elements considered.

System complexity (especially for 'Systems of Systems', which are discussed in Chapter 11) can require a certain number of iterations when initial results should be changed frequently due to requirement changes, availability of more accurate data or other system specific factors.

In LCC estimation, it may be recommendable to use a combination of different methodologies. Hereafter the most common analytical methodologies are described.

PARAMETRIC ESTIMATION

Parametric methodologies use algorithms called *Cost Estimating Relationships* (CERs) to estimate cost by applying statistical techniques (regression analysis) mostly relying on historical data.

CER is an equation that correlates characteristic system elements with corresponding cost elements; its choice should be appropriately derived from a correct application of valid data. CER validity should be checked from time to time on the basis of feedback from CER application to a certain system to be implemented.

The use of CERs in parametric estimation can be beneficial at the beginning of the system life cycle, since at this time there is insufficient information to support cost estimation, basically due to uncertainties in system characteristics, preventing an adequately accurate cost estimate. Nevertheless, the CER selection should be inevitably well-directed and satisfactorily justified, so as not to preclude the correct approach to the estimation process.

Further applications of CERs for parametric estimation are common in the area of software cost estimation. In certain instances, software cost can be considered as a (non-linear) function of the *Source Lines Of Code* (SLOC), however taking into account that, in this case, the resulting cost is essentially due to labour factors.

ANALOGY ESTIMATION

This is a case of 'indirect analysis', based on the correspondence with cost elements of an existing system showing specific similarities with the system to be estimated. This kind of estimation will require a technical and economic justification of the actual differences with respect to the existing system.

ENGINEERING (BOTTOM-UP) ESTIMATION

This methodology consists of a progressive aggregation of known or estimated cost elements that are located at a certain level of system breakdown. The total system cost is, therefore, evaluated in a bottom-up path, from a given level to the next upper level. This kind of estimation assumes that systems characteristics are known in detail, so that only at an advanced system implementation stage will an adequately accurate estimate be obtained.

Validation of LCC Estimates

Life Cycle Cost estimates are often reported to be unrealistic and, consequently, systems are likely to cost more than initially planned.

Validation of LCC estimates ensures that they are comprehensive, well documented, accurate, reliable and timely. These characteristics are reviewed hereafter.

COMPREHENSIVE ESTIMATES

Comprehensive cost estimates completely define the acquisition programme they are made for, reflect current schedule and are technically sound. Furthermore, the level of detail of the CBS, which LCC estimates are referred to, should be related to the purpose of definitely preventing omissions or double counting of cost elements.

WELL DOCUMENTED ESTIMATES

Rigorous documentation increases the integrity of estimates by identifying methods, calculations, outcomes, rationales or assumptions, and sources of the data used to generate each cost element.

Estimates should be correlated to system CBS and programme CBS. They should be documented in detail, with an indication of initial data, significance level and statistical test on CER. This will allow a reviewer to replicate the estimation process with the same results. Data should be traceable to the original documentation. CBS elements should be traceable.

ACCURATE ESTIMATES

Estimates are accurate when they are not overly optimistic, deriving from an evaluation of most likely costs and properly adjusted for inflation. In the event of changes in schedules or in other assumptions, estimates should always be revised to reflect their current status.

CERs and cost models need to be validated to demonstrate that they can predict costs within an acceptable range of accuracy. Before a parametric model is used to perform an estimate, the model should be calibrated and validated to ensure that it is based on current, accurate, and complete data and is therefore a good cost predictor. CERs that are utilized should be originated from regression processes requiring a good data interpolation, in which variances of values from the representative curve are minimized. Estimates should be really representative of most probable values, which in turn should be correctly correlated to their time of occurrence.

RELIABLE ESTIMATES

Justifiability is a key quality requirement of a good estimate. Key cost elements should be tested for sensitivity and the reasonableness of Ground Rules and Assumptions should be cross-checked to determine the reliability of LCC estimates. It is also important to identify limitations deriving from uncertainty or bias affecting data or assumptions.

TIMELY ESTIMATES

It is essential that the cost estimate be available in time to relevant decision makers. It is important to ensure that high-quality cost estimates are developed and delivered in time to support the decision-making processes. Estimates that comply with all the stated quality attributes may be of little use or may be overcome by events if they are not ready when needed. Timeliness is just as important as quality. Actually, the quality of cost estimates may be vulnerable if there is not enough time to collect historical data: since data are the key drivers of estimate quality, their deficiencies increase the risk that the estimate may not be reliable.

Good cost estimates are primarily based on firm requirements, access to high quality data and experience of cost estimators. Even with the best of these circumstances, cost estimating is not an easy task. Additionally, credible cost estimates take time to progress; they cannot be hasty. Their countless challenges increase the chance that cost, schedule and performance objectives will not be achieved. If cost estimators recognize these challenges and plan for them promptly, this can help organizations mitigate some of the potential risks of bad cost estimates.

The evolutionary acquisition system, mentioned earlier in this text, often makes cost estimating more difficult, because it requires that cost estimates be developed more frequently. In some cases, cost estimates made for acquisition programmes are valid only for the initial increment or spiral, because future increments and spirals are not the same product as they were at the outset. Nevertheless, unrealistic cost estimates may be avoided, resulting in more accurate long term investment funding and more effective resource allocation and increasing the chance that the programme will succeed.

In general, insufficient attention to LCC estimation can result in wasted money and time while compromising the quality of end system.

Concluding Review of Life Cycle Cost Analysis

A formal review of the LCC analysis might be necessary to confirm the correctness and completeness of results. The following steps are suggested in the aforementioned IEC standard:

a) Review of analysis objectives and scope, to ensure that they have been adequately defined and interpreted;

b) Review of LCC model (including cost elements definitions and relevant assumptions), to ensure its compliance to analysis purpose;

c) Review of application, to ensure that input data have been accurately defined, that the model has been correctly utilized, and the results (including sensitivity analysis) have been adequately appraised and discussed;

d) Review of all assumptions defined during the analysis process, with specific reference to their correctness and documentation acceptability.

A number of LCC studies take advantage of the availability of periodic updates to the LCC model they use, so that it becomes systematically applicable across the life cycle. For example, analysis is initially carried out on the basis of preliminary or roughly estimated data, but results can be updated as soon as more detailed data are available during the life cycle. Updated more accurate information might also affect modifications to CBS or estimation methodologies.

Effective management of decision-making processes across the systems life cycle is permitted by such pre-requisites as: the knowledge of actual system cost, the identification of costs for individual functional elements and, for specific life cycle tasks, the definition of major contributors to total cost and of the factors by which these contributors are determined, the assessment of risks associated with activities planned in different moments of acquisition, operation, maintenance and disposal.

Taking into account specific techniques by which cost categories and elements mostly affecting the total LCC can be identified in a CBS (that is, typically, in the acquisition phase, investments on facilities and fixed equipment and, as system operation starts, expenditures to keep the system efficient), analysts are frequently requested to determine likely causes generating these cost elements, in order to identify required precautionary measures.

Life Cycle Cost analysis is most efficiently applied in the initial life cycle phases, so as to optimize the overall system acquisition approach. Usually LCC analysis is based on an appropriate definition of assumptions for system design implementation, on a detailed identification of feasible technical solutions, on an accurate description of system operational requirements and logistic concept, on a satisfactory identification of critical *Technical Performance Measures* (TPM) and on a functional description of system configuration.

Nevertheless, it is often necessary to conduct LCC analysis iteratively, especially if estimated system cost is significantly affected by areas of uncertainty or risk.

Whether a formal application of LCC assessment process is required for a certain system, generally, depends on operational requirements and applicable instructions.

Still, LCC analysis provides beneficial elements for system decisions. It is worthwhile highlighting again that every decision on realizing a system may affect its performance, safety, reliability, maintainability, support and costs to produce and maintain the system. The basic Cost-Effectiveness target can be achieved through trade-off techniques, optimizing system characteristics (for example, its reliability) with respect to LCC.

According to the UK Ministry of Defence document *MOD Guide to Investment Appraisal and Evaluation*, optimism bias is defined as a demonstrated, systematic tendency for project appraisers to be overly optimistic. To redress this tendency, cost analysts should make empirically-based adjustments to the estimates of a programme costs, benefits, and duration. These adjustments should be based on data from past, similar programmes and should be calibrated for the unique characteristics of the programme at hand, in order to reasonably prevent uncertainties on cost values and, as a consequence, negative effects on the programme viability.

Realism and objectivity of cost estimates (along with lower risk/uncertainty margins) are based on rigorous adoption of estimation methodologies and computer models successfully applied in a large number of practical cases, through the professional commitment of worldwide specialists.

In summary, it should be remembered that an accurate estimate results from the systematic execution of estimation processes.

A number of important benefits will arise from a suitable approach to Life Cycle Costing; the most essential benefits being:

1.   Cost growth for different systems and different programmes will be efficiently managed.

2.   Cost estimates and forecasts will show increased accuracy and completeness.

3.   Accounting systems and data collection processes will be improved.

4.   Improved data availability will be advantageous in fund allocation for the acquisition of new systems.

Advanced and more complex systems are certainly beneficial to the achievement of some required performances, but, as noted by Blanchard, sometimes reliability and quality are weakened, and, as a consequence, long term costs tend to increase. Blanchard states that future systems should, therefore, be realized by balancing system cost and effectiveness aspects, *'as any specific design decision will have an impact on both sides of the balance and the interaction effects can be significant'*.

Besides the numerous benefits of Life Cycle Costing, there are also some major weaknesses. While current processes and practices are more oriented to the short term, successful implementation of the principles and concepts of Life Cycle Costing requires thinking and acting with a long term perspective in mind, so that highly advantageous results can be produced.

Cost visibility is a major requirement for increased life cycle management effectiveness and for a better utilization of financial resources. Implementation of more complex systems (and, especially, Systems of Systems), to comply with specific user needs, will lead to continuing refinements of LCC models for a better adaptation to the newer and future hardware/software architectures, in the framework of overall project management processes (planning, monitoring and control) and tools thereof, growing in importance along with evolving needs and objectives.

6

Selection of Computer-based Models for Cost Calculations

The Use of Computer-based Models in LCC Estimation

Computer-based models can be used in LCC estimation to identify costs that will be incurred in the implementation of a certain design solution and costs that can be saved (and possible revenues) as a consequence of this implementation.

Models adopted in estimating LCC elements should be selected to accommodate peculiarities and constraints specific to the system, so that design options can be thoroughly analyzed and especially certain details can be justified: for example, the maintenance concept optimization resulting from a Level of Repair Analysis (LORA).

As a general rule, it is advisable to use LCC models accounting for cost elements that best reflect the real system and its support scenario (also influencing system effectiveness), such as:

- Elements of system maintenance policy;

- MTBF data for an initial repair parts assessment;

- Cost of labour for scheduled and unscheduled maintenance in connection with maintenance requirements (MTTR and so on);

- Initial investment cost for support equipment, technical publications and training with reference to the constraints imposed by the organizational arrangement.

The advantage of such a breakdown is to apply predictive long-term estimation models using a limited set of essential parameters and simple analytical relations.

In this context, it should be emphasized that an optimum LCC value will be hard to determine mathematically. LCC models can be adopted, preferably, to compare alternative solutions, that is in a 'relative' rather than 'absolute' fashion.

LCC models to be used in computer processing are – by their nature – simplified representations of the real world. They extract main system characteristics and derive analytical expressions for cost evaluation (that is, the already mentioned Cost Estimating Relationships, or CERs) with reference to appropriate independent variables, to be selected on a case-by-case basis.

Commercial models exist in a large number to support LCC analysis models; other models are continuously being developed or updated. A comprehensive list of internationally used models can be found in the NATO Publication *RTO TR-SAS-054 – Methods and Models for Life Cycle Costing* (see Bibliography).

A suitable LCC model should comply with application-specific requirements, first of all as regards the comparison between different solutions for system/component implementation so that values of cost elements, significant for this purpose, can be quickly obtained.

Model quality can be appraised by the measure of such attributes as completeness, flexibility, repeatability of results and easy utilization. Analysts are required to become adequately familiar with the model functional mechanism, to assess its LCC analysis capability and especially to identify cost drivers in the Cost Breakdown Structure across the different system life cycle stages.

Usually, LCC models are designed for system applications on the basis of the following basic elements:

- User organizational procedures for technical and maintenance activities on systems;

- System utilization requirements;

- System logistic data base;

- Provisions for logistics support;

- Cost data base.

Realism of a LCC model is assured if:

- It represents system characteristics, including operational scenarios and maintenance concept;

- It is complete, with respect to the inclusion and prominence of all relevant LCC factors;

- It is simple enough to be easily understandable and applicable in decision-making processes, and also for the purpose of future adaptations and updates;

- It is designed to enable independent assessments of specific cost elements.

Simplest LCC models are essentially composed of a collection of algorithms for the estimation of costs associated to individual Cost Breakdown Structure elements.

The selection between in-house developed models and commercial models is related to analysis objectives, which should be satisfied on the basis of available data and of some other aspects including:

- The appropriate degree of selectivity to discriminate between different options;

- The degree of sensitivity required to obtain sufficiently accurate results;

- The duration planned for carrying out LCC analysis and presenting its expected results.

From Methodologies to Models

A cost model is a set of mathematical and/or statistical relationships arranged in a systematic sequence to implement a cost methodology in which outputs, namely cost estimates, are derived from inputs. These inputs comprise a series of equations, ground rules, assumptions, relationships, constants, and variables, which describe and define the situation or condition being studied. Cost models can vary from a simple one-formula model to an extremely complex model that involves hundreds or even thousands of calculations. A cost model is therefore an abstraction of reality, which can be the whole or part of a Life Cycle Cost.

It is essential that Life Cycle Cost models are able to support different types of analysis so that the decision-makers have a full understanding of the costs and the financial implications.

Specific risk areas may be explored by conducting a quantitative cost risk analysis, which could also be used to appraise overall exposures to risk in acquisition programmes.

All interested parties in the life cycle cost calculation have to agree on the use of common models. This will ensure that all subsequent calculations can be compared on an equal basis. The models should be either programme specific or COTS (commercial off the shelf), as required by the need of the programme.

In parallel to the selection of the models, a common CBS (Cost Breakdown Structure) should be defined for the programme. The results from the different models selected initially should be aggregated following the CBS defined above.

Once the models (with the way of aggregating their outputs) and CBS have been defined, the assumptions necessary to define the cost data should be commonly determined and agreed.

Cost Model Validation

The procedure described hereafter can assist in validating models, first by establishing qualitatively the model coverage and subsequently assess suitable measures of its comparative validity. The procedure is best used to appraise whether one model can be more useful than another, taking into consideration that its application to future projects will always imply some extrapolation beyond the original data set.

A model may include only cost estimating relationships originated by statistical analysis of the costs of the past projects and objectively connecting costs to specific quantitative design and/or performance features of the system. On the other hand, a number of models rely upon the subjective judgement of the user, so that their validation becomes impossible.

At the beginning of the validation procedure, it is appropriate to find a number of acquisition programmes whose costs can be used as references for the model being validated and that belong either to a well-defined class or to a generic class.

Regression (mostly *linear* regression) is then used to statistically correlate the actual cost as a function of the predicted cost. Regression parameters (number of observations, correlation coefficient and standard error) give an indication of the model performance.

Subsequently, the model is calibrated against new data, using output values of design and performance characteristics as inputs.

Prediction tests are more accurate than calibration. Here, output cost data not used previously are compared to the estimates made by the model based on simultaneous accounts of the performance and/or other characteristics of the acquisition programme at an earlier stage of its life cycle.

Similarly to calibration tests, the statistics of the cost estimating errors are evaluated. It may be difficult to find sufficient data to carry out an adequate prediction test since specialists tend to construct their cost models on all the programmes on which they have output data.

The following activities may be required whenever there is a need to assess the applicability of LCC tools:

- Analysis of available tools;

- Characterization of assessment indicators/criteria;

- Preparation of questionnaires and collection of information from software suppliers;

- Benchmark of commercial tools (features and potentialities);

- Selection of the most suitable tool.

Various challenges concerning the objective to provide a clear picture of the current status of commercial LCC tools can be identified as follows:

- Lack of sufficient data from model suppliers (model documentation);

- Lack of coordination between acquisition managers and model suppliers;

- Vagueness of questionnaires released to suppliers;

- Unavailability of licenses to evaluate the tools.

Certain features should be specifically considered in the assessment of LCC models. Work Breakdown Structures should be flexible enough to accommodate the necessary levels of detail, in accordance to decision-making needs and available data. Comparison with pre-existing LCC models will help correctly define the basic cost elements, to avoid the increase of the model's complexity due to redundant cost elements.

The parameters that define LCC elements should allow the use of mathematical functions and statistical distributions so that a range of acceptable numerical values can be established. The reliability of algorithms used should be confirmed on the basis of their outcomes. The user should be able to select the most suitable statistical distribution(s) for each cost element and to modify analytical expressions giving the estimated cost for a certain cost element.

LCC models should be capable of tracing the level of influence of individual parameters affecting each cost element to evaluate the parameter importance in the overall CBS framework. Furthermore, LCC models should be able to perform comparisons between their inputs/outputs and historical data or reference values, obtaining a more calibrated model and preventing errors due to an incorrect data introduction.

Another essential characteristic that provides additional flexibility to LCC analysis processes is the ability to compute LCC of elements using different operators (besides the four basic operations).

The ability to compute life cycle costs using variables with different weights can be helpful as the importance of parameters can be different during the period under consideration, also in accordance with the most suitable alternative as well as with users operational approach.

As life cycle cost calculations for a system can be computationally intensive, the model should be able to limit the computation time, allowing the user to perform only the minimum required analysis (for example by selecting specific periods and a limited set of alternatives).

Better calibrated LCC models and improved performances may be derived from optimization of model interactions with other software, like spreadsheets or more complex programmes intended for logistic design applications (RAMS = Reliability, Availability, Maintainability, Supportability).

The model should specifically incorporate provisions for a probabilistic sensitivity analysis of LCC parameters, in the context of risk analysis for cost estimation. This type of analysis leads to more effective results than a deterministic sensitivity analysis in evaluating the uncertainty inherent in the LCC governing parameters.

The identification of the cost drivers by the LCC model should be supported by different modes of presentation. Testing input data and tracking approximations in calculations should be possible in LCC models with the goal of providing more accurate LCC outputs.

Tools incorporated in the model should enable applications of financial and economic analysis techniques like net present value (NPV), discounted cash flow (DCF), internal rate of return of investments (IRR), asset and capital depreciation, opportunity costs, inflation, taxation, and other case-specific topics.

The following is a comprehensive scheme for the evaluation of model attributes; when developing cost models for generic applications these attributes would be desirable:

1.   General features:

   – User friendly interface;
   – Allows copy/paste functions;
   – Allows undo/redo functions;
   – Can manage different programmes at the same time;
   – Can compare different solutions in individual programmes.

2.   Main structures (CBS):

   – The model is flexible and easy to modify for each CBS element;
   – Allows drag-and-drop and cut-and-paste for copying and editing of CBS elements;
   – Allows graphical representation of CBS providing effective and fast data input and search;
   – Is able to perform comparisons with pre-existing LCC models to identify the basic cost elements;
   – Is able to create user subroutines (whenever necessary) for specific calculations;
   – Variables can be stochastic;
   – Is able to perform interactions between cost elements;
   – Cost functions changing over time can be defined;
   – The path of each cost parameter in the CBS can be traced;
   – The degree of parameters influence in each CBS element can be estimated;
   – Is able to perform comparisons between its inputs/outputs and historical data or reference values;
   – Is able to compute Life Cycle Costs using variables with different weights;
   – Is able to limit the computation time.

3.   Interaction with other software:

   – Can import data from MS Excel/MS Access/MS Project;
   – Can export data to MS Excel/MS Access/MS Project;
   – Imported data can be updated automatically.

4.   Data/Results accuracy:

   – Is able to perform sensitivity analyses;

    – Is able to perform risk analyses on LCC parameters;

    – Is able to notify the user if the alternatives considered have different levels of detail or different boundary conditions;

    – Is able to identify cost drivers and to provide reports with different modes of presentation;

    – Provides cost reports for selected combinations of Product Tree items and CBS elements;

    – Is able to immediately track errors in input data;

    – Is able to track errors in CBS equations.

The following topics should be considered as significant to differentiate the performance of the models:

- Ability to compare different alternatives in a single project;

- Ability to define cost functions changing over time;

- Possibility of tracing the path of each cost parameter of CBS elements and corresponding algorithms;

- Possibility of comparing inputs/outputs and historical data or reference values;

- Data import/export features;

- Ability to provide cost reports for both total and detailed costs for selected combinations of Product Tree items and CBS elements;

- Ability to track errors in input data and in CBS equations.

Some of the commercial software products that have been tested for the aforementioned features are the following: CATLOC (Systecon AB, Sweden), D-LCC (Decision by Life Cycle Cost – ALD, Advanced Logistics Development, Israel), Relex LCC (Relex Software Corporation, USA).

7

Conditions of Uncertainty and Risk in Life Cycle Cost Analysis

Definitions of Risk and Uncertainty

Hereafter a preliminary discussion is presented on the concepts of risk and uncertainty, two of the main elements that affect the accuracy of cost estimates. Risk and uncertainty are defined – for example, in the NATO Publication *RTO TR-SAS-069, Code of Practice for Life Cycle Costing* (see Bibliography) – in the following way:

- *Risk* is a measure of the chance that, as a result of adverse events, a certain point estimate (specifically, a cost estimate) will be exceeded. It is typically measured on the basis of two components, namely the probability of occurrence of adverse events and the consequences of these adverse events, should they actually manifest themselves.

- *Uncertainty* is the indefiniteness or variance of an event. It refers to all situations that are unpredictable, essentially due to lack of relevant information.

Frequently, both in specialized literature and in professional practice, the two terms risk and uncertainty are used interchangeably to mean an equal concept. Risk and uncertainty are logically correlated, for example by the assertion that *uncertainty generates risk*.

Basically, uncertainty is a situation in which a number of possibilities exist and it is unknown which of them has occurred or will occur. Risk is a characteristic of a situation in which a number of outcomes are possible, the outcome that will actually occur is uncertain and at least one of the possibilities is undesirable.

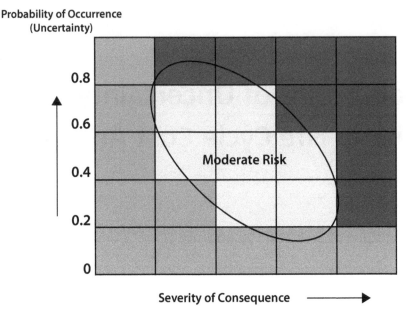

Probability of Occurrence
(Uncertainty)

0.8

0.6

0.4   **Moderate Risk**

0.2

0

Severity of Consequence ➔

Figure 7.1   Risk matrix

Figure 7.1 depicts a very common representation of risk as a function of probability and severity of the consequence of the adverse event. This is shown, for example, in the NATO Publication *RTO TR-SAS-054 – Methods and Models for Life Cycle Costing* (see Bibliography).

Regarding the Risk Matrix, however, a notable publication by the Association for Project Management (whose authors are recognized worldwide as experts on Risk Management) states that the matrix *'can lead to prioritisation outcomes that are not appropriate'*. Subsequently: *'For example, very low probability but very high impact threats may be given lower prioritisation than would be preferred'*. Therefore, appropriate caution is required in using the Risk Matrix (see Bibliography for further information).

As the probability of occurrence of an adverse event increases from 0 to 1, a classification in 5 levels can be envisaged, as depicted in Table 7.1, showing the different possibility to apply mitigating factors to control risk (related to the notion of *residual risk*).

At the same time, the severity of consequences can be categorized in five levels (Level 1, 2,…, 5) of growing severity, as illustrated in Table 7.2.

Table 7.1   Levels of probability for an adverse event

What is the likelihood the risk will occur?		
Level of probability	Explanation	Approach
1	Not likely	Risk can be effectively avoided or mitigated on the basis of standard practices
2	Low probability	Risk is mitigated by experience gained in corresponding cases with minimal oversight
3	Likely	Risk can be mitigated with some effort
4	Highly likely	Risk cannot be mitigated, a different known approach is required
5	Near certain	Risk cannot be mitigated; no known processes or approaches are available

Table 7.2   Levels of consequence for an adverse event

If the risk materializes, what would be the level of magnitude of impact?			
Level of consequence	Technical	Schedule	Cost
1	Minimal or nil	Minimal or nil	Minimal or nil
2	Minor performance losses, the current approach can be retained	Additional activities needed to meet key dates	Budget increase or unit cost increase lower than 1 per cent
3	Moderate performance losses, solutions available	Minor schedule deviations from required dates	Budget increase or unit cost increase lower than 5 per cent
4	Inacceptable performance losses, solutions available	Critical path of the programme affected	Budget increase or unit cost increase lower than 10 per cent
5	Inacceptable performance losses, no solution available	Key programme milestones cannot be achieved	Budget increase or unit cost increase higher than 10 per cent

At the launch of a system acquisition programme, and specifically in feasibility studies, LCC estimation plays a central role. As has been already stated, decisions taking place at the beginning of a programme may affect the programme cost to a larger extent. Later decisions have a decreasing incidence.

Based on this circumstance, programme cost management strategies shall take into consideration at an early stage Cost Risk Analysis models accounting for margins of indefiniteness inherent in LCC estimation, especially in the case of economically burdensome programmes.

The confidence level of LCC analysis results depends on the availability and efficient utilization of most significant information, on the assumptions of LCC model and on input data applied in the analysis.

Risk Management in LCC Analysis

The purpose of risk management is to identify, assess and mitigate effects deriving from any uncertain event that may occur and result in adverse consequences to a system acquisition programme (for example to system cost, schedule and technical characteristics). Risk management involves the work required to consider what can be done to reduce both the impact and the likelihood of the described risk, what are the trade-offs of the available options and what is the best way to address the described risk.

RISK PLANNING

Before risks can be identified, assessed and mitigated, a Risk Management Plan should be developed. This plan involves defining detailed activities to be accomplished by specific individuals within an established schedule.

Risk planning is the detailed formulation of a programme of actions for the management of risk. This process includes the following steps: development and documentation of risk management strategy; definition of the methods to execute the risk management strategy; planning for adequate resources. This process results in a Risk Management Plan (RMP).

RISK IDENTIFICATION

Identification of risk events is the act of determining and describing events that could impact the acquisition programme. These events are called risk items or risk elements.

Examples of common techniques for risk identification are workshops, interviews or brainstorming sessions.

After the risk events are identified, a risk watch list should be initiated. This list must be further refined during the later phases of the programme.

RISK ASSESSMENT

Risks are described by identifying what can go wrong, how it can happen, how it is likely and what is the magnitude of the adverse event should it actually happen.

Assuming the idea that a cost overrun, or an exceedingly high cost level, is the main event that can go wrong with a cost estimate, the first objective of the cost risk assessment is to identify what actually can go wrong. Cost overruns present understandable problems for cost estimators. Cost underruns do not have a similar impact, since the problems they present are different. Estimators are faced with the challenge of selecting a cost that has an acceptable probability of overrun without being so high as to preclude the economic feasibility of the programme.

The analysis of simulation results can help understand which of all the potential uncertainties affect total costs to the largest extent. In this sense, we can learn how costs can be higher than expected (that is, 'how it can happen'). Cost risk assessment offers opportunities to analytically test the assumptions and views about what is or is not significant in a cost estimate.

If knowing that something bad can happen is useful and knowing how it can happen is more useful, knowing how likely something is to occur is even more useful. A Monte Carlo simulation with 10,000 point estimates of costs may yield a cost distribution that addresses this question. There are several different approaches: for example one could consider a specific cost level, like £10 million, and ask the likelihood of it being exceeded; or a specific value might be selected because it may represent the maximum investment that is economically feasible, or a cost ceiling for the programme, or else a maximum amount that a sponsor is willing to spend. With 10,000 cost estimates, it is possible to answer most reasonable questions about the likelihood of any particular cost arising; it is simple to calculate the number of costs that were less than or equal to £10 million or any other selected value. The observed frequency becomes the estimate of the probability that such a cost is not exceeded.

As regards the consequences of a cost overrun, its size may lead to economic disbenefits, to loss of support from the sponsor or to a need to have the programme re-authorized. Selection of contingencies is a common way of managing the risk of exposure to cost overruns, accounting for the uncertainty in cost estimates. The more the contingency, the less likely a cost overrun will be; however, the benefits of lower impact and likelihood of overruns are not without their costs. While using a higher contingency prevents cost overruns, the final choice will be influenced by the risk appetite of the sponsor.

Estimates of cost, schedule and system performance are always affected by subjective elements leading, in specific cases, to wider or narrower ranges of variation for numerical values, which in turn give rise to uncertainty factors.

The probability theory is the conceptual foundation of estimation methodologies. By applying the concepts of random variables, it is possible to determine the functional relation between cost values within a certain range and respective probability.

RISK MITIGATION AND TRACKING

Risk mitigation means reducing the likelihood of occurrence or severity of its consequences, or both. There is usually a trade-off to be made between the magnitude of the risk and the resources needed to reduce that risk to an acceptable level.

Each of the risk events is placed in one of three conditions (high, medium or low). The boundaries of these categories are typically stated in the Risk Management Plan. The appropriate risk mitigation action varies with the level of risk.

Risk mitigation strategies can be selected among the following: reduction (reducing the risk impact or probability, shifting the risk timeframe, or changing the risk's consequence); investigation (conducting research until a decision on a mitigation approach can be made); acceptance of the risk by doing nothing (anticipating that the risk may have to be managed in the future); tracking the risk and its attributes for early warning signs of critical changes.

Risk tracking involves watching the risk elements identified and the mitigation results both internal and external to a project. The evaluation of the progress, and effectiveness, of risk mitigation actions is monitored by comparison of the predicted results with the actual performance.

Sensitivity Analysis

In principle, sensitivity analyses should be included in all cost estimates because they evaluate the effects of changing ground rules and assumptions.

Since uncertainty cannot be avoided, it is necessary to identify the cost elements that represent the most risk and, if possible, to quantify the risk. This can be done by performing both a sensitivity analysis and an uncertainty analysis.

Sensitivity analysis helps select the most appropriate alternative. Actually, for a sensitivity analysis to be useful to decision makers, it is necessary to assess carefully the underlying risks and supporting data. In addition, the sources of the variation should be well documented and traceable.

Sensitivity analysis reveals how the cost estimate is influenced by a change in a single assumption when the effect of changing one assumption or cost driver at a time is considered, while holding all other variables constant. Hence, it is easier to identify which variable has most effect on the cost estimate.

Irrespective of whether the analysis is performed on only one cost driver or several within a given scenario, the difference between sensitivity analysis and risk or uncertainty analysis is that sensitivity analysis attempts to isolate the effects of changing one variable at a time, while risk or uncertainty analysis observes the effects of many variables changing simultaneously.

Sensitivity analysis involves recalculating the cost estimate with different quantities for selected input values, or parameters, comparing the results with the original estimate. If a small change in a value yields a large change in the overall cost estimate, the results are considered sensitive to that parameter. As a result, helpful information can be provided by sensitivity analysis since it highlights elements that are cost sensitive. For example, assumptions and cost drivers having the greatest influence on the LCC estimate may require further reconsideration to ensure that the best possible value is used for that parameter. If the LCC estimate is found to be sensitive to several parameters, all the assumptions should be reviewed, to ensure that sensitive parameters have been thoroughly explored and the best possible values have been used in the final point estimate.

SENSITIVITY FACTORS

Uncertainty about the values of some, if not the majority, of the technical parameters is common early in the life cycle of systems. Many assumptions made at the beginning of a programme turn out to be inaccurate.

Some factors that are often varied in a sensitivity analysis are: the duration of system economic life; the potential requirements changes; the configuration changes; the alternative programme assumptions; the changes in performance characteristics.

Many factors that should be evaluated are defined by the assumptions and performance characteristics delineated in the technical baseline and in ground rules and assumptions. Sensitivity analysis should include the assumptions that are most likely to change.

BENEFITS AND LIMITATIONS OF SENSITIVITY ANALYSIS

Sensitivity analyses grant access to cost values ranging from a best case to a worst case. It is often preferable to know the range of potential costs around a point estimate and its underlying reasons than to simply rely on a point estimate. Sensitivity analyses can clearly reveal both the high and low costs that can be predicted.

Sensitivity analyses also provide an unambiguous picture of critical assumptions and cost drivers that most affect the results, giving additional information for the final decision-making process. Sensitivity analyses enable decisions that influence the whole system life cycle by identifying the elements that have the greatest effect on cost.

Cost Risk Estimation Process

Cost Risk models extend the applicability of parametric models based on algorithms relating cost to quantitative system characteristics. The degree of inaccuracy induced by probabilistic cost estimation methods can be reduced by adopting methods such as the Three-Point methodology, which will be discussed later, or more sophisticated techniques.

An even better result can be obtained by an appropriate combination of these kinds of methodologies with simulation methodologies. As mentioned previously, a well-known family of simulation models is Monte Carlo, based on the use of random sampling to address a certain problem, either probabilistic or deterministic.

Monte Carlo simulation assesses the overall uncertainty inherent in a model. It calculates the model iteratively using randomly selected values from the error distribution for each of the model components and then using the set of results from all the iterations to estimate the distribution of the overall model results. The Monte Carlo method has been successfully used in scientific applications for over 60 years after its invention attributed to Stanislaw Ulam, a Polish-born mathematician (1946).

Probability distributions of variables of an uncertain or random nature (that is, *stochastic* variables) can be combined in a large cost model for a system acquisition programme to obtain a total cost probability distribution.

Data collection and analysis represents the most essential part of the cost risk estimation process. It is also a critical step in the process. All variables in the cost estimating model potentially affected by risk and uncertainty first need to be identified. These variables often include simple ratios and factors as well as more sophisticated CERs based on regression analysis.

Probability distributions need to be estimated or selected for each variable. This requires first selecting the type of distribution to apply and then estimating the distribution's parameters such as high, low and most likely values.

Historical data may provide a useful source of information on risk and uncertainty for use in the cost risk assessment applying, for example, least squares regression analysis to generate the input to the Monte Carlo simulation. Historical data have been traditionally used in probability estimates, with some difficulties regarding the data selection process.

Expert judgement is often applied whenever relevant historical data are scarce, for example if the systems under study represent new concepts and technologies for which little or no experience exists. In other terms, expert judgment may be suitable if data are uncorrelated or not easily available, if they are too expensive to access, if their interpretation is ambiguous.

The details of cost risk estimation are discussed, for example, in the NATO Publication *RTO TR-SAS-054 – Methods and Models for Life Cycle Costing* (see Bibliography). A summary of the procedure is described below.

Following the data collection and analysis process, a *baseline cost estimate* is generated using Monte Carlo simulation. To generate a baseline cost estimate, a fixed value for the cost driver (that is, the independent variable) is fed into the CER; a similar process is followed for other CERs. Costs are aggregated for all CBS elements and the procedure is repeated for several times until a baseline cost estimate emerges.

The baseline estimate is used to account for uncertainty in the correlation between dependent and independent variables in each CER. Limitation of available data and human randomness and errors may contribute to this uncertainty.

Subsequently, a *risk-adjusted* cost estimate is generated. At this stage, cost drivers (independent variables) are no longer considered as deterministic, but stochastic. Typically, distributions for these parameters are triangular.

While the baseline cost estimate contains modelling uncertainty, the risk-adjusted cost estimate contains both modelling uncertainty and technical uncertainty and risk, which means that the risk-adjusted probability distribution has a higher mean value and a higher variance than the baseline estimate. The difference in mean (expected) values of the two distributions defines *cost risk*.

The Three-point Method

The simplest way to represent risk/uncertainty conditions is the triangular probability distribution function, which is applied in the three-point method for cost estimation.

This can be used when there is reason to believe that some values in an interval are more likely than other values and it is thought that there is a most likely value (representing the mode, or most frequent value, of the statistical distribution), so that the estimator can use the minimum, most likely and maximum values to identify the triangular distribution.

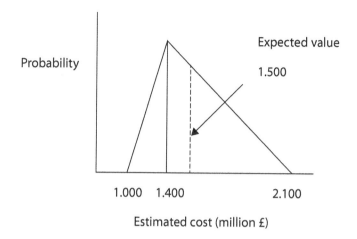

Figure 7.2   Three-point method for cost estimation

In Figure 7.2, these values are respectively £1.0, £1.4 and £2.1 million, so that an expected value can be calculated as the arithmetic mean of the three values:

$$\frac{1.0 + 1.4 + 2.1}{3} = 1.5 \ \text{£million}$$

The variance σ^2 of this distribution is the following:

$$\sigma^2 = \frac{1.0^2 + 1.4^2 + 2.1^2 - 1.0 * 2.1 - 1.0 * 1.4 - 1.4 * 2.1}{18}$$

$$\sigma^2 = 51{,}666.67 \ \text{£million}^2$$

Following the same procedure, it is also possible to conduct quantitative risk analyses and sensitivity analyses, in order to improve decision-making processes under the stated uncertainty conditions.

Although the choice of the minimum, most likely and maximum values is essentially subjective, nevertheless it provides a certain degree of flexibility (and realism) with respect to a single point estimate; the latter furthermore results in a smaller accuracy.

CBS element cost probabilities are combined to develop an overall programme cost estimate probability distribution. However, simply adding (*rolling-up*) the most likely CBS element costs does not result in the most likely cost estimate because the risk distributions associated with the various elements are different.

Therefore, it may be appropriate to create statistical probability distributions for each CBS element or risk by specifying the risk shape and bounds that reflect the relative spread and skewness of the distribution; the probability distribution represents the risk shape, and the tails of the distribution reflect the best and worst case outcomes.

Because different CBS element costs may be affected by the same external factors, some degree of correlation exists between them. Correlation identifies the relationship between CBS elements so that when one WBS element's cost is high within its own probability distribution, the other WBS element will also show a high cost in its own probability distribution.

Monte Carlo simulation can be efficiently used to combine the individual cost elements and their distributions. The cumulative probability distribution resulting from the Monte Carlo simulation provides risk-adjusted estimates and corresponding probabilities. The output of the simulation is useful for determining the level of probability in achieving a point estimate, along with a range of possible outcomes bounded by minimum and maximum costs.

Uncertainty analysis using a Monte Carlo simulation communicates the likelihood of a programme being completed. It may also determine how different two competing alternatives are in terms of cost. In addition, estimating future costs with probabilities is always better than just relying on a point estimate.

To identify which CBS elements may need contingency reserve, uncertainty analysis can be used to prioritize risks, based on probability and impact affecting the cost estimate. Knowing which risks are important will drive the allocation of contingency reserve.

PART TWO

Detailed Approach – Selected Applications

8

Criteria and Methodologies for Life Cycle Cost Estimation

All good things which exist are the fruits of originality (John Stuart Mill)

Overview of Life Cycle Costing Concepts

As discussed earlier, Life Cycle Costing concepts can be successfully applied in the evaluation of alternative system configurations, alternative manufacturing processes, alternative support policies, and similar decision-making processes. LCC analysis provides a cost-effective solution on the basis of figures of merit directly associated with LCC, through iterations affected by interconnected technical and economic factors intended to minimize the total cost. The ultimate solution will be satisfactory especially if sufficient attention is paid to cost factors since the very beginning of the system life cycle, despite the obvious fact that the majority of system costs are incurred later, namely during and after the Production Stage.

It has also been emphasized that the future cost commitment is largely defined during the Development Stage and prior to production, in which timeframe critical decisions significantly affect the LCC. This should be appropriately considered on the basis of the inevitable degree of approximation of initial LCC estimates.

Trade-off Tools for Life Cycle Costing

Trade-off studies for Life Cycle Costing are concerned with the quantification of different options (in terms of cost, planned schedule, risks and performance levels) to ensure that a successful system configuration is conceived. Comparison between options is typically based on LCC values, for a better arrangement of different life cycle phases, taking systematically into consideration both technical and economic issues and carefully monitoring system effectiveness in correlation with cost, especially with reference to In Service Support for its entire duration.

LCC Estimation Processes: Application Criteria

LCC estimation processes involve a set of tasks to be performed systematically:

- Estimation process planning;

- Data investigation, collection and analysis;

- Development of estimation arrangement;

- Determination of estimation methodologies;

- Determination of estimated cost;

- Presentation of estimate for decision-making processes.

Each of these tasks is discussed hereafter.

ESTIMATION PROCESS PLANNING

At the beginning of estimation process, the tasks to be performed are planned in accordance with overall requirements for LCC estimation. Process definition and planning include: information on the final use of estimate; identification of the required level of detail; overall description of the system for which the LCC estimate is needed; definition of ground rules and assumptions; selection criteria for estimation methodologies; preparation of the plan arranging for all preliminary elements required for an effective estimation process.

DATA INVESTIGATION, COLLECTION AND ANALYSIS

In view of subsequent application of appropriate estimation methodologies, an early appraisal of available data is necessary to support the selection of most suitable methodologies. If the application of a parametric method is envisaged, the development of Cost Estimating Relationships (CERs) will have to be considered, taking into account all consequences in terms of model design schedule, accuracy verification and confirmation of applicability to the specific case.

Alternatively, if the direct application of historical data from similar programmes is deemed possible, preliminary verification of available data is required to confirm that these data are actually applicable. This preliminary verification can be supported by appropriate assessment criteria based on previous experience, extrapolations and – if it is conceptually correct – normalizations.

DEVELOPMENT OF ESTIMATION ARRANGEMENT

The arrangement of LCC estimation essentially reflects the CBS (following, in turn, the original WBS), taking into consideration the first level of cost elements: initial acquisition costs (denoted as LCCA), ownership costs (LCCO) and retirement costs (LCCR). As the life cycle proceeds, it will be possible to explore in more detail the comparison between estimated costs and actual costs.

DETERMINATION OF ESTIMATION METHODOLOGIES

As will be explained in more detail in this chapter, various methodologies are available for cost estimation. Therefore the selection of the most appropriate methodologies is of primary significance to meet estimation quality objectives. For this purpose, it is also advisable – and often beneficial – to utilize more than a single methodology, in order to improve the accuracy of the estimation process.

DETERMINATION OF ESTIMATED COST

Estimation of a numerical cost value derives directly from the foregoing stages of the LCC analysis process and from the topics discussed in the previous sections of this book. Applicable computer-based models can be used to carry out the calculations required.

PRESENTATION OF ESTIMATE FOR DECISION-MAKING PROCESSES

Once an estimated cost value has been calculated, the results of LCC estimation process will have to be presented for management review and approval, which implies that all estimation process steps have been unambiguously considered and documented.

Estimation documentation is a reliable indicator of good estimation performance. This is a primary concern for decision makers who rely on estimation results.

Basic Estimation Methodologies

Ideally, cost estimation should be initiated early in the system life cycle, where the highest influence on the overall cost outline is possible.

If sufficient historical data are not available and suitable for use in an indirect cost estimation process based on analogy for an acquisition programme, it will be necessary to utilize direct estimation processes based on parametric methodologies to obtain an expected cost.

In addition, each system is characterized by specific Technical Performance Measures (TPM), allowing correlation between estimated costs and respective performance levels.

In selecting an estimation methodology, it should always be considered that cost estimation is a guess of future costs based on straightforward criteria for the assessment of available data, which basically drive the selection. Relevant selection criteria are the level of acquisition programme definition, the required level of detail and the estimation schedule constraints. It is also meaningful to correctly appraise, whenever applicable, the impact of such components as *Commercial Off-The-Shelf* (COTS) and *Non-Developmental Items* (NDI), frequently influencing the estimation accuracy and the corresponding uncertainty of cost calculation. Another factor to be considered is the degree of innovation of the system.

As regards the aspects of the level of definition of the system acquisition programme and of the required level of detail, when a typical innovative programme is initiated, the level of definition is generally far from being satisfactory with respect to the wide range of alternatives for system requirements implementation. These conditions lead to the choice of suitable parametric models, which are applicable in the presence of very scarce information.

Once the design baseline has been defined in more detail and more programme information has become available, the parallel use of analogy estimation could be advisable. At a later stage, when prototypes or pre-production samples will have been manufactured, 'Engineering' or 'Bottom-Up' methodologies are applicable, on the basis of an aggregation of elementary cost data, allowing cost estimation of higher level elements in the CBS. Again, it is necessary to take into account the incidence of COTS and NDI elements in the design of new systems, wherein integration costs and other cost factors (for example, due to performance critical or safety critical system aspects) can have some impact.

With reference to schedule constraints for the estimation, the preference of parametric methodologies can be driven by lack of available time. Higher levels in the CBS are addressed first.

Specific estimation methodologies are reviewed in the following paragraphs, expanding the previous discussion in Part One.

PARAMETRIC COST ESTIMATING METHOD

Parametric methods use statistical relationships between historical costs and programme, physical and performance characteristics.

Examples of physical characteristics used as independent variables for parametric estimating are weight, power and software lines of code. These variables should be cost drivers of the programme, whose sources can be found, for example, in the technical baseline. The underlying assumption is that the same factors that influenced cost in the past will continue to influence future costs. This method is often used when little is known about a programme.

Applications of parametric methodologies require access to historical data, which sometimes are difficult to collect. Parametric estimation is driven by data from many programmes and covers a broader range.

Having created a statistically effective cost estimating relationship on the basis of historical data, the parametric CER can be used to estimate the cost of the new programme by entering its individual characteristics into the parametric model. CERs established early in the life cycle of an acquisition programme should be regularly revisited to ensure that they are current. In addition, parametric CERs should be well documented, since severe estimating errors can happen if the CER is misused.

Parametric relationships originated from statistical analysis can be used to provide a confidence level for the estimate, based on the predictive ability of the CER, which relies on historical data ensuring objective results. This increases the credibility of the estimate.

Data normalization can be a lengthy process, including verification that the data were normalized accurately. CERs should be properly updated to represent the current state of the cost, technical and programme data. Analytically complex CERs (for example, nonlinear CERs) may lead to difficult interpretation of the relationship between cost and its independent variables.

In the electronics area, for example, system cost is proportional to the number of components in the system. A limited number of components may produce favourable effects on such characteristics as weight, reliability, safety, leading ultimately to economic benefits in the system life cycle implementation (actually, across all stages before and during production and subsequently in Utilization, Support and Retirement Stages).

Parametric techniques are also significantly helpful in shortening the estimation process. Even in more complex cases, parametric methodologies effectively support the identification of cost impacts deriving from design enhancements, schedule variations and technical modifications.

ANALOGY COST ESTIMATING METHOD

This method takes into consideration that no new acquisition programme represents a completely new system. There are programmes originated from an adjustment or an evolution of previous programmes; there are systems derived from new aggregations of existing components or sub-assemblies. This provides means to enable cost estimation both at individual component level and at sub-system or system level, based on actual updated costs taking into account different complexities, technical designs, physical configurations or other programme/system characteristics.

The analogy method can be used before detailed programme requirements are known. If the analogy is strong, the estimate will be credible. The connection to historical data is simple and can be quickly understood.

Analogy relies on a single data point. It is always necessary to find the detailed cost, technical and programme data required for analogies; this, sometimes, can be difficult. Analogy also relies substantially on expert opinion to apply the existing system data to the new system; nevertheless, subjective judgements should be avoided whenever possible.

The main reason leading analysts to the choice of analogy-based models is that cost data that are available for a detailed analysis may be incomplete, combined with the presence of similar and known systems, that can be considered for comparative purposes. This comparison may involve functional, dimensional, structural or technical design characteristics. Technical specialists will ensure that the analogy is accurate and that the tailoring is correct; cost estimates will be more reliable if the extent of such an investigation can be expanded down to sub-systems and cost elements of sufficiently low level.

The required technical review of analogy accuracy could pose some challenges to specialists, thereby representing a limitation of the analogy method. In addition, it is firmly required that cost data, on which the comparison and the subsequent estimate are based, are actually available. Two kinds of purely technical factors can interact in association with this purpose, namely complexity factors and miniaturization factors. In accordance with the concept of complexity discussed in previous sections, this is influenced by differences in design and performance features; miniaturization (typically for aircraft and electronics) accounts for the fact that, for a certain performance level, the smaller a device, the more expensive its manufacture.

ENGINEERING (BOTTOM-UP) COST ESTIMATING METHOD

The engineering (Bottom-Up) cost estimating method builds the overall cost estimate by aggregating detailed estimates performed at lower levels of the CBS.

The application of this method assumes the availability of detailed data on system configuration, which will have been collected until the system reaches an advanced life cycle stage. This enables dealing with cost elements sufficiently well-defined and realistic.

Large amounts of data are needed to estimate labour and material costs accurately, taking into account relevant estimated needs, particularly in the case of COTS components.

This estimating technique provides cost analysts with the capability to establish accurately what is included in the estimate and if anything was overlooked. It also gives good insight into major cost contributors.

However, this method can be expensive and lengthy to implement; it is not adaptable enough to answer what-if questions; it requires new estimates to be built for each alternative; it also poses difficulties in reflecting changes in the estimate.

COMBINED ESTIMATION METHODOLOGIES

It is the cautious practice of cost analysts to perform cost estimates by utilizing at least two different cost estimation methodologies. Estimates, therefore, typically derive from a combination of methodologies.

Since each individual cost estimation effort has its own peculiarities, a combination of methodologies enables greater flexibility in estimation processes. Basic selection criteria are, essentially, the same as already discussed:

- level of acquisition programme definition;

- required level of detail;

- availability of necessary data;

- schedule constraints for the estimation process.

REQUIRED COST ESTIMATE UPDATES

Every time the programme scope is modified, cost estimates need to be updated. Cost estimates are made for all programme alternatives in order to determine the cost impact of alternative solutions, so that decision-making processes based on economic considerations can be streamlined.

Example of a Generic Cost Breakdown Structure

We now consider a generic detailed example of CBS. It should be noted that there may be extreme differentiations in the arrangement of life cycles for the numerous conceivable systems, also depending on the system application scenarios.

The first level breakdown of our system encompasses the following main cost elements:

- Initial acquisition cost (LCCA). This includes unit system costs from Concept Stage to Production Stage.

- Ownership cost (LCCO). This is composed of unit costs for Utilization Stage and Support Stage (which proceed in parallel and can be grouped together to form an In-Service Stage).

- Retirement cost (LCCR). This includes unit cost for system disposal and associated tasks required by safety regulations.

Life Cycle Cost is therefore given by:

$$LCC = LCCA + LCCO + LCCR.$$

At the second level breakdown, costs for Concept Stage to Production Stage are shown as components of LCCA:

$$LCCA = C_C + C_D + C_P$$

In this equation, C_C includes costs for ensuring the feasibility of the system, which means that the system can be developed, produced, operated and maintained at an affordable cost and quality. C_C can be obtained by the following equation:

$$C_C = C_{CR} + C_{CA} + C_{CS} + C_{CM}$$

C_{CR} are costs for market research, not including costs related to marketing and selling the system.

C_{CA} are costs for system concept and design analysis. These costs incurred for conceiving a system that is expected to meet user demands can vary significantly whether, for example, system concept is a variant of a proven concept or an entirely new one to be developed. C_{CA} typically includes costs for basic research, for technology selection, for initial concepts of operation, for preliminary design engineering (covering architectural design, interfaces design, reliability, safety, electromagnetic compatibility, climatic and environmental compatibility) and for system/subsystem demonstrators.

C_{CS} are costs for preparing specifications of user requirements to ensure efficient system utilization over its lifetime.

C_{CM} are costs for the management of Concept Stage.

At the second level, the cost for Development Stage (C_D) includes costs for designing and developing a system that meets the specifications and customer expectations and costs to provide proof of compliance. C_D is given by the following equation:

$$C_D = C_{DD} + C_{DS} + C_{DT} + C_{DV} + C_{DP} + C_{DE} + C_{DQ} + C_{DM}$$

C_{DD} are costs for design engineering, continuing the preliminary work done during the Concept Stage (cost element C_{CA}) to refine system characteristics and configuration details for the design of architecture, interfaces, hardware, software, firmware (if present).

C_{DS} are costs for preparing the necessary documentation for the design effort during the Development Stage.

C_{DT} are costs related to performing the necessary test programme on the system in order to ascertain system conformity (in its prototype configuration and down to component level) to regulatory requirements for type approval, also regarding safety, environmental and electromagnetic compatibility and so on.

C_{DV} are costs for selecting suppliers of components complying to system design among those vendors that are qualified as preferred suppliers.

C_{DP} are costs for manufacturing prototype systems and/or subsystems intended to validate system design characteristics prior to entering Production Stage.

C_{DE}, corresponding to Producibility Engineering, includes costs for analysis of design alternatives to estimate the manufacturing costs for each alternative and associated risks.

C_{DQ} represents costs for ensuring that all activities carried out during the Development Stage are effective and efficient with respect to system quality and performance.

C_{DM} are costs for managing the development work.

For Production Stage, C_P includes both recurring costs and non-recurring costs related to system manufacture and delivery, taking into account the required number of systems to be delivered to users: $C_P = C_{PR} + C_{PN}$

Recurring costs can be categorized as material costs (C_{PRM}) or processing costs (C_{PRL}).

Material costs include all direct material that is used in delivered systems and material that is scrapped during system manufacture ($C_{PRMD} = C_{PRMDU} + C_{PRMDS}$); they also include all indirect material allocated to manufacture (C_{PRMI}).

Processing costs account for direct work hours and rework hours ($C_{PRLO} = C_{PRLOD} + C_{PRLOR}$), and also machine hours, both direct and rework hours ($C_{PRLM} = C_{PRLMD} + C_{PRLMR}$). Clearly, rework hours are indicative of inefficiency.

In Appendix 1 we will discuss the applicability of the theory of Learning Curves, typically in the case of extended series production, which may progressively affect the amount of recurring costs: the reduction of these costs directly derives from the decrease of processing hours as a function of the number of items (systems) in the series.

In the case of non-recurring costs, cost elements to be considered are generally the following:

- Costs for Producibility Engineering (C_{PNP}), due to adaptation of production processes and design tuning to minimize manufacturing costs.

- Costs for qualifying vendors of components to become preferred suppliers (C_{PNV}).

- Investment costs (C_{PNI}), for the procurement of production equipment (C_{PNIE}) and manufacturing test equipment (C_{PNIT}), the construction of facilities (C_{PNIC}) and the procurement of tools and equipment for installation (C_{PNII}).

- Costs for documentation of the production processes and installation procedures (C_{PND}).

- Costs for training of personnel to perform the production and installation operations (C_{PNT}).

Subsequently, we consider the second level elements of *ownership cost* (LCCO), namely costs for Utilization Stage (C_{OU}) and concurrent Support Stage (C_{OS}). Generally these costs, as a whole (that is, as In-Service costs), include one-time fixed investment costs (C_{OI}) and annual variable expenses, which can be quantitatively expressed by an annual average value (C_{OY}) times the number of years N that the ownership cost is incurred (N * C_{OY}).

Investment cost C_{OI} can be further broken down into: cost for investment in spares (LRUs, LRPs and consumables); cost for investment in maintenance equipment, instruments and tools (i.e. *Special-to-Type Test Equipment*, STTE); cost for investment in personnel training; cost for investment in documentation; cost for investment in facilities required for storage, transportation and so on.

Therefore the following equation applies:

$$C_{OI} = C_{OIS} + C_{OIE} + C_{OIT} + C_{OID} + C_{OIX}$$

Specifically, the spare package might have to be fairly extensive to minimize the risk of obsolescence; accordingly, the numerical value of C_{OIS} becomes higher. If an unexpected situation of obsolescence occurs, the system may have to be redesigned, causing higher investment costs.

Annual cost C_{OY} can be broken down into the following components:

- Annual cost for personnel training (C_{OYT});

- Annual cost for preventive maintenance, based on average labour estimation (C_{OYP});

- Annual cost for corrective maintenance and repair of LRUs, based on an estimated number of repairs per year and on estimated average labour (C_{OYR});

- Annual cost for consumables and used LRPs (C_{OYC});

- Annual cost for spares handling and management, based on average labour estimation (C_{OYO});

- Annual cost for storage of spares (C_{OYS});

- Annual cost for transportation of spares (C_{OYN});

- Annual cost for utilities, for example water, energy and so on (C_{OYX});

- Annual costs for having the system supplier solve technical problems remotely or on-site (C_{OYE}).

For commercial systems, it may be appropriate to add the estimated cost of unavailability over the system life cycle. The impact of an unavailable system will be different depending on the specific situation, but whatever the case actually is, system unavailability could lead to loss of income for the user.

Finally, costs for *Retirement Stage* can be broken down into: (1) Costs for system shutdown (C_{RS}); (2) Costs for disassembly and removal (C_{RD}); (3) Costs for recycling and safe disposal (C_{RR}); (4) Retirement management costs (C_{RM}).

The following equation applies:

$$LCCR = C_{RS} + C_{RD} + C_{RR} + C_{RM}$$

9

LCC Evaluation for System Software

Fundamentals of Software Cost Estimation

The importance of software components in systems is significantly increasing in current acquisition programmes. Consequently, it is appropriate to identify universal criteria for the assessment of LCC for system software, to ensure that cost estimates are realistic and complete.

Estimating software development can be difficult and complex; the achievement of successful completion of software development projects on time and on budget can be difficult and complex.

Capers Jones, the well-known software expert, emphasizes *'the frequency with which large software projects fail, and the even larger frequency that have cost and schedule overruns'* (see Bibliography). This is one of the main reasons why initial software estimates should be sufficiently accurate and not overly optimistic.

In common with typical system (hardware) cost estimating procedures, in the case of software estimation, the purpose of the estimate and the estimating plan should be defined first, then software requirements and development effort should be defined, ground rules and assumptions should be established and, subsequently, a point estimate should be developed. Obviously, sensitivity analysis should be carried out as part of the overall risk and uncertainty assessment effort. Updating final estimates with actual costs is also relevant for software cost estimation.

Comprehensive approaches to software production cost estimation and life cycle processes are provided by Londeix and Sommerville (see Bibliography).

Londeix states that ('*as costing is the purpose of estimating*') an estimating method is successful when:

- The early estimate is within ± 30 per cent of the actual final cost.

- The method allows refinement of the estimate during the software life cycle.

- A higher accuracy can be achieved by monitoring and re-estimating the development each time more information is available.

- The availability of tools increases the effectiveness of the method, mainly because results can be obtained more quickly and in a standard fashion.

In turn, according to Sommerville:

- Software costs often dominate system costs. The costs of software on a PC are often greater than the hardware cost.

- Software costs more to maintain than it does to develop. For systems with a long life, maintenance costs may be several times development costs.

- Software engineering is concerned with cost-effective software development.

The papers and presentations by Capers Jones mentioned in the Bibliography section give further insights and references on software cost estimating.

Uniqueness of Software Characteristics for Cost Estimation

Unlike hardware, software changes constantly, so that good data collection for cost estimating is subject to uncertainty constraints. Software is primarily labour-intensive and development effort is typically non-recurring.

How much effort is needed to develop software depends on its size and complexity; these main cost drivers are also in common with hardware development. Software cost estimation is based on two main elements: the software to be developed and the development effort required to be undertaken.

Manual Estimates

The utilization of resources, time and funds can be predicted by means of the traditional aforementioned methodologies: analogy, bottom-up or parametric (the latter using appropriate Cost Estimating Relationships).

Manual estimates can perform the estimate rapidly and easily, but they are not particularly accurate.

Tool-based Estimates

Tools for software development cost estimation are well suited to satisfy the requirement for accurate and reliable estimates. There are hundreds of acquisition programmes that witness the successful outcome of tool-based software cost predictions, taking advantage of an inherent flexibility of use. This benefit is typically counter-balanced by the effort expended for users to become adequately familiar with the tools, involving also a certain amount of training costs.

Quantification of Software Development

Prediction of software size is usually the first step of a software estimation process. Estimating software size depends on scope, complexity and interactions of software functions. Evolution of requirements and scope contributes to size and to the consequential cost and schedule estimates.

In the development of new (or partially new) system software, cost estimation is directly correlated to software size; Source Lines of Code (SLOC) or Function Points (FP) are common measures of software size.

Source lines of code (SLOC) is a software metric measuring software size on the basis of the number of source code lines. The objective of this metric is to establish software complexity and to estimate resource requirements for software production and maintenance. SLOC count is useful to define an order of magnitude for the code, but not to provide an accurate measurement for the software project under consideration: it would be meaningful to use SLOC count to compare a 10,000-line project with a 100,000-line project, not to compare a 20,000-line project with a 21,000-line project. The origin of SLOC-based metric dates back to traditional line-oriented languages (FORTRAN, Assembler, C). In these cases, SLOC count actually gave a genuine representation of software complexity, which is no longer true with current object-oriented paradigms. It is clear, however, that SLOC-based code complexity metric is the easiest to measure and to implement. These characteristics help maintain the SLOC technique (which was originally made popular by COCOMO and, thereby, incorporated into many costing tools) in common usage, although defining a line of code has been found difficult due to conceptual differences involved in accounting for executable statements and data declarations in different languages.

On the other hand, for various reasons, SLOC-based metric seems to be no longer suitable at present: as recently stated by Capers Jones, '*Unfortunately lines of code is not a valid metric and cannot safely be used for estimation*'. This caveat is a valuable confirmation of the fact that a combination of estimating methods is generally required – or, at least, highly advisable – for software development cost estimation.

Function points were introduced by IBM in the early 1980s. This approach employs user interface features to estimate program size. It is the most common technique for estimating management information system (MIS) application size. Object metrics have become feasible only with the popularization of object oriented development and use objects as a predictor of programme size.

Function Point metrics can take advantage of the existence of well-established standards and of their regular update. These metrics are logical and simple, and can be widely applied across the entire life cycle. They are independent from technologies, platforms and languages; their applications have a high degree of conformity and objectivity from the user point of view.

Instead, one should consider that the impact of manual operations in the Function Point process is high and that deep knowledge of standards is required. Additionally, the availability of historical data may be rather poor.

Estimating Software Development Effort

After completing the initial software sizing, an estimate of software development effort can be originated in terms of the human resource requirements. Differences in activities can significantly affect overall costs, schedules and productivity rates and, therefore, it is critical to properly tailor activities to the type of software project being estimated.

To convert software size into software development effort, the size is usually divided by a productivity factor (as mentioned before) such as number of source lines of code, or function points, developed in a given period of time. This productivity factor depends on several aspects: for example, the language used; the application of new or reused code; the skill of developers; the development tools used.

When a productivity factor is used, all parameters associated with its evaluation have to be taken into account. After selecting the productivity factor, the corresponding labour hours can be obtained, on the basis of an assumed number of productive hours per day and of days per year for the developers.

Scheduling Software Development

Estimating the schedule for completing the software development work is part of the overall software estimation process. Software development schedule can be significantly influenced by such factors as requirements evolution or the extent of quality control. As regards the human factor, it is alleged that, if more developers are added to an existing team, its members are increasingly less able to work effectively: as stated by Brooks, '*adding manpower to a late software project makes it later*'.

Large software development efforts frequently experience schedule delays and, therefore, cost increases, particularly due to complications in the management of software configuration and team communications, affecting in turn software management and design effort. Minimizing the time for requirements analysis can influence the quality of the software developed.

It cannot be assumed that software will be delivered with no defects, so that rework should be accounted for in the schedule, along with the time and resources related to problem analysis, code redesign and test re-iteration.

Software Maintenance Costs

After installation in its planned location, software undergoes periodic maintenance. Costs for software maintenance activities have to be accounted for in the LCC estimation, differentiating between *corrective maintenance* (costs for removal of defects not revealed in previous tests), *adaptive maintenance* (costs for software compliance to external changes and technology improvements) and *perfective maintenance* (costs for adding new functionalities or enhancements).

The level of maintenance to be expected depends on several factors, primarily on software complexity. Additional perfective maintenance may be needed in case of modifications to requirements. The amount of corrective maintenance is affected by the extent and completeness of previous software tests.

Parametric Software Estimation

Parametric tools can be used to estimate the cost for software development and maintenance. Parametric tools rely on historical data collected from a number of previous projects providing cost, schedule, effort and risk estimates generally regarding software size, development environment, percentage of code reuse, programming language, personnel skills and experience and labour rates.

Parametric tools are particularly beneficial in the early stages of the software life cycle, when requirement specifications and design are still unclear. Using these tools in software development can help identifying potential problems early enough to alleviate their impact.

When a software project matures and actual data become available, the accuracy of the cost estimates produced by a parametric tool is typically likely to improve. To ensure this, tools should be calibrated with actual data, leading to more accurate estimates.

Software Cost Risk Analysis

When a Cost Risk Analysis is incorporated in the software cost estimation processes (for example, in the aerospace applications), inputs for cost estimation may derive from the following factors:

- requirements

- architectural design

- mission/project schedule

- implementation approach

- mission/project WBS

- software implementation and design approach.

In turn, some constraints exist, for example, as a consequence of applicable processes and procedures and of design principles adopted in software development.

Software cost metrics archives can be useful in supporting the initial estimates of software size and effort, on the basis of the collection and analysis of technical and programmatic requirements and of the subsequent definition of work elements.

After the effort is scheduled and a first cost estimate is developed, the impact of risk should be determined and models and/or analogy are used to enter risk elements in the cost estimation. The estimation process is then completed by the review and approval of the estimate.

Typical Software Life Cycle Cost Breakdown

In a typical software life cycle, the main cost drivers can be identified as follows: human resources, software maintenance and modifications (or redesign) due to poor product quality.

Across a typical system software life cycle, cost breakdown occurs in accordance with the approximated percentages mentioned in Table 9.1 below.

Table 9.1   Example of software LCC breakdown

Generic software life cycle phases	Estimated cost by phase
Concept and definition	2 per cent
Requirements definition	4 per cent
Software architecture design	7 per cent
Software detailed design	6 per cent
Code and unit testing	7 per cent
Integration and system testing	12 per cent
Acceptance testing	3 per cent
Preparation for delivery	1 per cent
Delivery, installation and training	2 per cent
Maintenance	55 per cent
Retirement	1 per cent

Additional Remarks

As stated by Capers Jones, 'large software projects are among the most risky business ventures in history. The failure rate of large systems is higher than other kinds of manufactured products. Cost overruns and schedule delays for large software projects are endemic and occur on more than 75 per cent of large applications.' In addition, 'the software industry also uses metrics that violate standard economic principles and distort results in very significant ways. The two most common flawed metrics include "cost per defect" which penalizes quality, and "lines of code" which penalize high-level programming languages.'

According to Capers Jones, software cost elements for large applications in descending order of cost influence are:

- Defect removal (inspections, testing, finding and fixing bugs);

- Producing paper documents (plans, specifications, user manuals);

- Meetings and communication (clients, team members, managers);

- Programming;

- Project management.

In order to apply standard economics principles to software development, Capers Jones suggests that '*it is of considerable importance to be able to measure productivity and quality using standard economic principles. It is also of considerable importance to be able to predict productivity and quality before major projects start.*'; and recommends: '*Given the economic importance of software, it is urgent to make software development and maintenance true engineering disciplines, as opposed to art forms or skilled crafts.*'

According to Capers Jones, the process of software cost estimation, as typically performed by software estimating tools, is composed of the following eight steps: sizing project deliverables; estimating defect levels and removal efficiency; selecting project activities; estimating staffing levels; estimating effort; estimating costs; estimating schedules; estimating requirements changes during development.

For example, the cost of a software activity is related to effort and personnel cost but is subject to extreme variations across industries or geographic areas. Schedule estimation is strongly correlated to cost estimation and is also subject to large variations.

Several books and publications of which Capers Jones is the well-known author describe in detail the use of software metrics and especially the implications of software economics. Some of the most recent publications are listed in the Bibliography for further insights into this matter.

10

Applications of 'Activity Based Costing' Concepts

Fundamentals of Activity Based Costing

In traditional volume-based costing systems – mostly utilizing volume related allocation bases – costs are traced on the basis of the structural level of the organization at which costs are incurred. This traditional approach, in which cost objects consume resources, is still considered as the most familiar costing system and relatively easy to implement. In the case of direct labour intensive processes that are characterized by high material costs and low overhead costs (that is, those costs that are not included as direct labour or direct materials), this approach is reasonably accurate; this is not true anymore when overhead costs and capital costs become higher.

Activity Based Costing (ABC) considers the activities performed and the causes of these activities. Activity is intended as any combination of personnel, technology, materials, processes and environment that produces a given system or service.

A causal relationship is recognized between costs of resources, activities and the cost objects: cost objects consume *activities* which, in turn, consume *resources*; in other words, costs are traced through activities to cost objects following a two-stage process. The first stage traces costs from the organizational budget to activities that are assigned to resources (labour, materials); in the second stage, activity costs are traced through the activity cost drivers to the cost objects.

The difference between the traditional costing system and the ABC system is schematically illustrated in Figure 10.1.

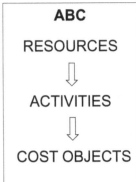

Figure 10.1   Traditional Costing and Activity Based Costing Systems

Having defined a reference object for which cost is to be determined (that is, the *cost object*), the following step of the ABC procedure is the identification of activities corresponding to this cost object. The intensity of activities is influenced by cost drivers, representing a key aspect of the ABC procedure. Cost drivers establish a connection between each activity and the cost object.

Activity cost is determined as the sum of costs of resources that are consumed by this activity.

There are several categories of costs that must be captured and identified for the activity model. Each of these categories presents different characteristics and behaviours that will affect its use.

For example, personnel cost is the most significant variable expense of an organization. It will individually account for 60 to 80 per cent of the total organization's costs. Labour, luckily, is also one of the easiest costs to trace to organizational elements because of the method in which people are assigned to do work. Due to its potential impact on decisions within each activity, it is important that this cost estimate be as accurate as possible. There are two data components of the labour force to be determined, number of employees and cost of labour. Both of these factors will be important at different times in the evaluation process. Direct labour costs will be the most easily assigned.

As ABC practitioners know, since costs are not deterministic in nature, it is impossible to calculate a cost accurately because cost estimates depend on the choice of activity drivers, activity definitions, and so on. Furthermore, costs cannot be managed unless we understand the underlying drivers.

In ABC systems, essentially, costs are not considered either variable or fixed on the basis of a production volume, but in accordance with the complexity and differentiation of production range. Following this perspective, variable costs become more numerous than those considered by the traditional approach, since the differentiation entails costs for a number of activities.

These costs, while traditionally considered as *fixed costs*, are also *indirect costs* with respect to their allocation. Moving from a short-term perspective to a long-term one, these costs become *long-term variable costs*, due to the length of the period between the decision to incur such costs and the moment in which the effects of this decision are revealed. This situation justifies the term *long-term variable costs*.

As a whole, an ABC system is a primary element for the enhancement of cost management systems. In fact, it supports accounting information systems in effectively analyzing the organization operations.

The following didactic example shows that the results obtained by using the traditional accounting system and the ABC system can be different.

Let us suppose that two products are manufactured by a company: Product A and Product B. The following data are considered:

	Product A	Product B
Production volume	2,000	10,000
Unit production time	5 hours	4 hours
Annual production time	10,000 hours	40,000 hours

For each production unit, direct material and labour costs are:

	Product A	Product B
Direct materials	25	17
Direct labour (6.00 £ per hour)	30	24

Total production fixed costs amount to £800,000 per year. These costs are apportioned to six company activity centres as follows:

Activity centre	Activity driver	Apportioned cost	Activity driver quantity per product		
			Product A	Product B	Total quantity
Assembly	Direct labour hours	80,000	10,000	40,000	50,000
Machine set-up	Number of set-ups	150,000	3,000	2,000	5,000
Quality control	Number of controls	160,000	5,000	3,000	8,000
Management of work orders	Number of orders	70,000	100	300	400
Storage	Number of stored items	90,000	150	600	750
Production overhead costs	Machine hrs consumption	250,000	12,000	28,000	40,000

Let us consider the following assumptions:

1. The company apportions total fixed costs to products on the basis of direct labour hours.

2. The company apportions total fixed costs to products using activity centre costs.

In cases 1 and 2, we wish to determine unit production costs for Products A and B and subsequently to compare the results.

CASE 1

Initially, direct costs have been given for Product A and Product B. Now we need to identify indirect costs, in order to find unit costs for the two products.

If we divide the total production fixed costs by the total production hours per year, we obtain the following hourly rate:

$$\frac{800,000}{50,000} = 16 \text{ £/hr}$$

Since the unit production time is five hours for Product A and four hours for Product B, unit indirect costs for the two products are:

16 * 5 = 80 £ for Product A

16 * 4 = 64 £ for Product B

Unit costs, including both direct and indirect costs, are therefore:

	Product A	Product B
Direct materials	25	17
Direct labour (£6.00 per hour)	30	24
Total direct costs	55	41
Indirect costs	80	64
Total unit costs	135	105

CASE 2

The activity costing rate will be calculated first, on the basis of the ratio of activity costs to total activity driver quantities:

Activity centre	Apportioned cost	Total driver quantity	Activity costing rate
Assembly	80,000	50,000	£1.60/hr
Machine set-up	150,000	5,000	£30.00/set-up
Quality control	160,000	8,000	£20.00/control
Management of work orders	70,000	400	£750.00/order
Storage	90,000	750	£120.00/storage item
Production overhead costs	250,000	40,000	£6.25/machine hr

Having calculated activity costing rates, it is possible to apportion indirect costs to the various activities, using activity drivers for each of the two products:

Activity centre	Product A		Product B	
	Activity driver quantity	Apportioned cost	Activity driver quantity	Apportioned cost
Assembly	10,000	16,000	40,000	64,000
Machine set-up	3,000	90,000	2,000	60,000
Quality control	5,000	100,000	3,000	60,000
Management of work orders	100	17,500	300	52,500
Storage	150	18,000	600	72,000
Production overhead costs	12,000	75,000	28,000	175,000
Total fixed indirect costs		316,500		483,500

Therefore, for the production volumes of 2,000 for Product A and 10,000 for Product B, the unit production cost can be calculated for the two products:

	Product A	Product B
Direct materials	25	17
Direct labour	30	24
Total direct costs	55	41
Indirect costs	185.25	48.35
Total unit cost	240.25	89.35

CONCLUSION

The results obtained from the two approaches are different. Following the traditional (*Full Costing*) approach based on direct labour hours, a larger amount of unit costs has been charged to Product A (£135), which requires more unit production time with respect to Product B (£105). In the case of ABC, Product A again presents the higher unit costs (£240.25) with respect to Product B (£89.35) because indirect costs are higher.

The Concept and Approach of Activity Based Life Cycle Costing

Activity Based Life Cycle Costing (ABLCC) is a forward looking life cycle approach to cost management. It is a cost prediction system, introduced by Emblemsvåg in his book '*Life-Cycle Costing. Using Activity Based Costing and Monte Carlo Methods to Manage Future Costs and Risks*' (see Bibliography), which is based on a specific definition of resources, activities and cost objects.

ABLCC applies simultaneously the ideas of Life Cycle Costing and Activity Based Costing to effectively manage system lifetime costs in uncertain conditions, by means of the concepts of *activity drivers* and *resource drivers*. Resource drivers keep track of how activities consume resources; activity drivers describe how cost objects consume activities. Both resource drivers and activity drivers are used to successfully capture the '*cause and effect*' relationship between activities (namely, what is actually being done) and cost objects. Costs are apportioned according to this relationship; Figure 10.2 describes the different treatment of direct costs and indirect costs in accordance with a typical ABC approach.

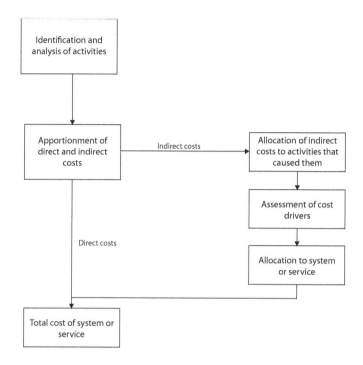

Figure 10.2   Stages of Activity Based (Life Cycle) Costing

Activity Based LCC can in many ways be considered as a synthesis of Activity Based Costing (ABC), LCC, and Monte Carlo methods. While ABC identifies the causal relationships of cost drivers to activities, Activity Based LCC – as an 'offspring' of ABC – is in fact a Life Cycle Costing analysis and not just a cash flow analysis.

While, in Life Cycle Costing analysis, cost estimation often represents the most challenging task, the lack of good historical data upon which accurate estimates can be based is a common problem. In many instances, the more traditional short-term-oriented accounting data have been used as a source, but a data collection capability enabling a long-term functionally-oriented cost evaluation is not in place. Applying the principles and concepts of ABC is essential in the tracing of costs back to their different causes and the responsible functional elements of the system. Full cost traceability is, therefore, essential if it is required to properly assess the risks associated with usual design and management decision making associated with the implementation of acquisition programmes.

In the aforementioned book, Emblemsvåg illustrates the following ten steps describing his ABLCC approach:

1.   Define the scope of the model and the corresponding cost objects.

2.   Obtain and clean Bill of Materials for all cost objects.

3.   Identify and quantify the resources.

4.   Create an activity hierarchy and network.

5.   Identify and quantify resource drivers, activity drivers and their intensities.

6.   Identify the relationships between activity drivers and design changes.

7.   Model the uncertainty.

8.   Estimate the Bill of Activities.

9.   Estimate the cost of cost objects and their performance measures (that is, Economic Profit).

10.   Perform Monte Carlo simulations and relevant analyses (such as sensitivity analysis and cost-effectiveness analysis).

In Step 1, it is crucial to realize that, since the product properties are established early in the product life cycle yet have large consequences for the entire life cycle, the Activity Based LCC model must include *all* applicable processes. To give decision support with respect to organizational issues, the model must therefore treat every activity as a cost object.

As regards Step 2, Emblemsvåg states that, for an activity based approach to function well, it is important that the Bill of Materials '*does not contain any overhead costs that are not volume related in order to reduce possible distortions to a minimum*'.

In Step 5, '*the purpose of resource drivers is to trace how the activities consume resources, while activity drivers are to trace how the cost objects consume activities.*

When identifying these drivers, it is crucial that they are chosen to represent as closely as possibly the actual consumption as described by cause-and-effect relationships. That is, the drivers are to represent cause-and-effect relationships between activities and resources and between cost objects and activities'. In addition, *'two types of consumption intensities exist: fixed and variable. A fixed consumption intensity is a consumption intensity that does not vary as the magnitude of the drivers (such as the material prices) changes. This is typically the case for direct costs. A variable consumption intensity, in contrast, varies as the magnitude of the drivers varies, such as the machine-hour price'.* The choice of the drivers may be influenced by the ease of obtaining data required by each driver and by the correlation between the consumption of activities implied by each driver and the real consumption.

In Step 8, *'to estimate the cost of an activity, the resource driver is multiplied by its consumption intensity. This is done for all the activities and is then summed up to produce the total cost of all the activities, which is the Bill of Activities (BOA)'.*

The difference with respect to the subsequent Step 9 *'is that in Step 8 resources are traced to activities, whereas in this step activity costs are traced to cost objects'.*

Finally, in Step 10, the uncertainty in the model can be handled by using commercial cost risk software such as Crystal Ball software. Furthermore, this can be employed to trace the critical success factors. The Crystal Ball software performs the Monte Carlo simulations. The sensitivity analysis measures statistically how the uncertainty of the different assumption cells affects the uncertainty of the forecast cells using rank correlation as measure. The assumption cells with the largest absolute magnitude of the correlation coefficient are the most critical success factors.

Activity Based LCC approach is different from the traditional LCC approach, although both rely on cost estimation across the life cycle of systems. While traditional LCC is typically structure oriented (for example, based on Cost Breakdown Structures), ABLCC is process oriented and, for example, views fixed costs and variable costs from a different perspective with respect to the traditional view.

The incorporation of Monte Carlo methods is an essential feature of Activity Based LCC. As a consequence, uncertainty is effectively taken into account; in addition, critical success factors can be successfully identified by using the recognized drivers to improve the life cycle cost effectiveness of systems.

Advantages and Disadvantages of Activity Based Life Cycle Costing

There is little doubt that one of the main advantages of ABLCC is that decision makers are provided with the relevant information they need to make better decisions. ABLCC incorporates all costs, all cost objects, all activities, and therefore it offers, basically, a complete cost picture.

On the other hand, ABLCC also has disadvantages. One disadvantage is that ABLCC requires more data than the traditional LCC approaches, because ABLCC includes a complete process perspective. Another is that even though it is more logical than other LCC approaches, it is not always easy to find a suitable balance between the level of detail and the convenience of the details.

While, generally, ABC techniques are considered not suitable for costing during the early life cycle stages, their adoption across later stages is aimed at improving cost estimating accuracy, especially if overhead costs play a primary role over the entire amount of system costs.

11

Economic Aspects of 'System-of-Systems Engineering'

Fundamentals of System-of-Systems Engineering

According to the *International Council on Systems Engineering* (INCOSE), the definition of System-of-Systems (hereinafter SoS) applies to a system-of-interest whose system elements are themselves systems; typically these entail large scale inter-disciplinary problems with multiple, heterogeneous, distributed systems. These interoperating collections of component systems usually produce results unachievable by the individual systems alone.

As a result of the technological evolution of systems, Systems Engineering has ultimately evolved into System-of-Systems Engineering to design and manage the integration of a complex set of component systems working together to provide capabilities not delivered by any single component system within the SoS architecture. The key architecture feature in a SoS is the framework supporting the integration of existing and new component systems. The characteristics of this architecture determine the easier or less easy integration of SoS component systems in and after initial development.

In specialized literature, different definitions for SoS can be found, on the basis of the scope of possible SoS applications, basically reflecting three elements: products (namely, the characteristics of SoS architecture), processes (design/integration/test) and personnel (lead system integrator, namely an organization that oversees the definition, development and integration of a SoS).

In a SoS structure, every system has the capability to operate in a stand-alone mode, and also to contribute to the achievement of higher level mission requests. Life cycles of individual systems may show some differences, since integrations or replacements of system elements can take place in order to meet system requirements. If these requirements are taken into consideration, then the effects of integration between different SoS elements have to be properly evaluated in each specific case.

SoS Engineering is different from the usual Systems Engineering. For example, if we consider a SoS as composed of interdependent systems connected to provide a given performance, losing part of the system will cause a significant performance degradation of the entire SoS. In addition, while the SoS activities are similar to more traditional Systems Engineering activities, the length, breadth, depth, and associated complexities are much greater.

An example of a system of systems would be an aircraft. While the aircraft may be developed as a single system, it could incorporate subsystems developed for other aircraft (for example, the radar from an existing aircraft may be incorporated into the aircraft being developed rather than developing a new radar), so that the new aircraft can be considered as a SoS composed of the airframe, engines, radar, avionics and all other elements necessary to meet the aircraft capability requirements.

Another specific example, in the broad range of defence applications of Systems of Systems, is the current development of Open Systems Architectures, which – due to their inherent flexibility – are deemed to yield innovation, reduced cycle time, and lower total ownership costs.

From a general Systems Engineering point of view, the implications of a SoS, compared to 'elementary' systems, may typically refer to the following specific attributes: broader technical scope, greater complexity of integration efforts, dynamic and challenging design (especially as regards risk/uncertainty issues and to the emphasis on design optimization), re-configurability of system architectures; peculiarity of SoS simulation and modelling; rigorous interface design and management.

Approach to System-of-Systems Costing

The perspective of 'System-of-Systems thinking' supports system engineering techniques useful for conceiving and designing large and complex projects; these techniques must, of course, include the consideration of life cycle costs.

The realization of every SoS involves trade-offs between different solutions and between individual systems performance. From a costing perspective, one of the specific challenges is the achievement of an optimum trade-off between cost and functionality, performance and dependability across the System-of-System as a whole. This optimum trading may take place in parallel for each of the component systems and these are individually optimized; however, the overall trading at the System-of-Systems level doesn't always happen. The underlying reason is often related to schedule constraints during system design / detailed design and to the need to accommodate long-lead procurement.

From an economic point of view, the selection of applicable cost models has been found to be influenced by a number of discriminating criteria, a few of which are deemed essential: the SoS stakeholders, the SoS architecture and its lead system integrator(s), and the degree of system component independence in terms of activities required in the life cycle stages for each component. This means that, in order for a cost estimation model to be effectively useful in SoS estimates, it is essential to look first at organizations requiring this sort of information for their strategic goals, especially the system purchasers and its user communities. Secondly, having identified a lead system integrator, this will be responsible not only for selecting SoS architectures but, thereafter, for supervising integration and test activities representing significant cost elements. Furthermore, the degree of independence of Life Cycle Management activities at component level is expected to influence the selection of cost models applicable to system software and to the remaining elements of SoS Cost Breakdown Structure, taking care to possible cost overlaps and double countings.

The economic aspects of System-of-Systems Engineering are based on the development of cost estimates mainly using a combination of parametric and bottom-up methodologies.

At the beginning of the life cycle of a SoS, parametric techniques are generally used for cost estimation. These techniques rely on a quantification of the size and complexity of the SoS to be delivered; size is driven by weight for hardware and by source lines of code or function points for software. Design process and organizational factors drive complexity.

An example of parametric cost model is COSYSMO (Constructive Systems Engineering Cost Model), introduced at the University of Southern California to estimate the system engineering effort, which is used in combination with

PRICE H and SEER-H to extend the estimate to hardware development costs. COSYSMO follows a parametric modelling approach used to estimate the quantity of systems engineering labour, in terms of person-months, required for the initial life cycle stages until the deployment of large-scale software and hardware segments in a SoS. In his book, Farr (see Bibliography) provides a more detailed description of how COSYSMO is used to carry out SoS cost estimates, while advising on its shortcomings: for example, since the model is developed on the basis of historical data, Farr states that the analysis of these data requires specific significant experience.

COSOSIMO (Constructive System-of-Systems Integration Cost Model), another current parametric model from the University of Southern California, includes activities such as the definition of the SoS architecture, the solicitation and procurement process for the SoS components and the integration of the SoS components into the SoS framework.

While COSYSMO estimates the systems engineering effort associated with system development or system modifications required to enable the SoS architecture (this effort is typically performed by independent organizations responsible for the component systems), COSOSIMO estimates the effort associated with designing the SoS architecture communications mechanisms, protocols, and interfaces, as well as the effort required to integrate, tune and test the SoS architecture.

In COSOSIMO, cost and size factors are related to the SoS high-level architecture, the processes used for design and integration/test and the experience and capabilities of lead system integrator.

Inputs to COSOSIMO are also scale factors: level of maturity of the SoS architecture; efforts to reduce cost and schedule; integration risk factors; maturity level of the system components and number of major component system changes; readiness of component systems for integration; capability of integration team; maturity level of integration processes.

In later life cycle stages, parametric cost estimates can be combined with bottom-up estimates following the hierarchical SoS structure (hardware and software architecture 'building blocks') that is being gradually defined, from low level components upwards. This work is typically reflected in the form of a Work Breakdown Structure (WBS), which makes this estimate easily justifiable because of its close relationship to the activities required to realize the SoS. This can translate to a reasonably accurate estimate at the lower level.

More accurate cost estimates are related to the definition of architectures in which SoS components can be designed or modified with a low degree of interdependency; this will reduce the level of risk in using current systems engineering practices and software development cost models. However, since SoS development efforts usually span many years and include many incremental or evolutionary iterations, long term estimates are generally impossible.

Specifically:

- The existence of SoS means that it is necessary to consider the life cycle costs of component systems as inter-related.

- The nature of these relationships is primarily dependent on the procurement strategy and the support strategy and this makes the estimation of the life cycle costs more uncertain.

- It is essential to consider that indirect costs are probably not unique to any one component system (for example, transportation costs and storage costs may be shared).

One key point is that most of the costs of many large scale systems will occur after delivery of the SoS to the customer. The supply chain issue – single or multiple suppliers – is one of the issues; in addition, when dealing with 'long-life' systems (aircraft, ships and so on), it is inevitable that there will be obsolescence issues to deal with; another issue is the choice between cheap components that fail more frequently with respect to more expensive components that demonstrate greater reliability.

System-of-Systems Cost-effectiveness

Assessing the effectiveness of a SoS with respect to its life cycle cost becomes an increasingly challenging problem. Demands for increased performance, lower system life cycle costs, longer operational capabilities and improved productivity and efficiency must be balanced against limited resources, partial and sometimes unknown data, the identification and resolution of conflicts and problems and resource allocation.

System/SoS effectiveness is related both to performance and especially to its ability to complete its mission in accordance with its operational requirements and at an affordable life cycle cost. Typically, decisions are requested in order to solve one of two problems:

- maximization of the SoS performance subject to a cost constraint;

- minimization of additional costs under performance constraints.

The former is applicable to the acquisition of a SoS – in the first part of its life cycle – whereas the latter arises in the utilization and support of the SoS.

Upgrades can be made by adding new types of systems to a SoS (this adds functionality and also an opportunity to insert advanced technology). Another possibility is to procure additional quantities of existing component systems (for an increased scope and capability of the SoS). A third option is to replace obsolescent or ageing component systems.

Measures of Effectiveness (MOEs) and Measures of Performance (MOPs) are common metrics used to characterize a SoS. The high-level SoS requirements that are relevant to its entire mission generate several MOEs, related to individual functions of the SoS mission; MOEs are, therefore, quantitative (but sometimes qualitative) evaluations of what a SoS should do in response to its intended mission. A MOE may be a measurable quantity or calculated from other output parameters, or it can also take the form of a weighted combination of several other metrics.

In turn, each MOE generates several MOPs that quantify the SoS response to requirements. MOPs can take different forms, such as:

- simple counts or measures (for example, the number of failures occurred in a certain period of time; the time elapsed until the occurrence of a failure; the time needed to repair a failure);

- averages (for example, the mean time between two consecutive failures);

- rates (for example, the number of failures occurred for each year of operation);

- percentages (for example, the percentage of failures that resulted in shutdowns).

Conclusions

When designing a solution to deliver a SoS capability, it must not only meet all performance requirements, but it must do so within affordability constraints. All possible solutions should be focused on the specified constraints for stated key performance parameters (KPPs). No solution should be presented that does not satisfy these constraints. Component systems that drive performance considerably above specified performance in these areas should be carefully scrutinized as well. All possible solutions should first be validated to ensure that they successfully address all KPPs and support all operational situations.

When new component systems must be developed to deliver some currently non-existing capability or degree of performance, it is important to get the most from the technology investment.

Attempts should be made to incorporate as much capability as practical into the new development to reduce the number of different component systems.

Increases in complexity associated with technology readiness and component stability may be counterbalanced by size decreases if the number of required component systems can be reduced. At the same time, care should be taken to ensure that expectations for technology do not exceed practical limits on innovation imposed by schedule constraints on the programme.

Carefully planned architectures with simple communication protocols that meet many different needs will reduce the size of the SoS solution space. Despite the investment needed to accurately design the SoS architectures and to standardize communication protocols, the payoff can be considerable across the life of the SoS.

Emerging requirements will result in the addition of new component systems that must communicate with existing components. The use of COTS hardware and software is a practical and necessary approach to accomplish the delivery of SoS capabilities in required timeframes.

Cost drivers for a SoS fall into two categories: those that define the size of the system engineering tasks, and those that drive the complexity of the engineering and management tasks. A crucial issue is the requirement for increased involvement of systems engineering resources throughout the life cycle of the SoS. Systems engineers are involved in requirements elicitation and management, architecture decisions, test and evaluation, verification and validation and technical oversight.

Risk management becomes of special importance when dealing with a System of Systems. Risk management efforts in a SoS should be hierarchical, where each system element implements its own risk management and communicates its findings and activities to appropriate higher level SoS risk management functions. The highest level SoS risk management function coordinates risk management activities across the entire SoS and, more importantly, oversees the risks associated with the interfaces and interactions of the individual system elements in the SoS. These latter risks are often not visible to the individual system elements. This is another reason why it is so important to deal with these system family issues appropriately.

Appendix 1
Application of Learning Curve Concepts in Life Cycle Cost Evaluation

Foreword

Drawing attention to the need for more accuracy in cost estimates, quantitative elements for the calculation of time to manufacture a given system, in a medium to large scale production, and of consequent cost, using a classic Learning Curve (LC) approach, are given hereinafter with a view to the possibility of assessing the impact on the system Life Cycle Cost.

It should be noted that, in concept, the Learning Curve is not a continuous line, since the production quantities (that is the values in horizontal axis) are integer numbers only, so that in graphical representations dotted lines should be drawn.

The Learning Factor in the Determination of Unit Production Costs

It is commonly known that the amount of direct labour hours is affected by the progressive learning of skilled operators who repeatedly perform the same sequence of activities. As a consequence of learning, the number of direct labour hours required to manufacture a certain assembly decreases significantly as experience is gained in production and the rate of reduction of assembly hours declines with rising cumulative output.

This means that, as production quantities vary, the average unit time will vary and, therefore, the cost will also vary. The average unit cost will tend to lower values.

In order to accurately evaluate the average cost of a certain system, on the basis of the total quantity to be produced, it is necessary to take into account the law of reduction of average manufacturing time as production quantity increases.

Experience in series productions has indicated that a correlation may be established between the reduction of manufacturing times and the quantities produced; this provides a useful tool to help in predicting manufacturing times along the series and estimating correlated costs.

The quantitative correlation may be expressed in terms of unit cost learning curve or cumulative average unit cost learning curve, with the following difference:

- The unit cost is an instantaneous value at any point during the extended production sequence;

- The cumulative average unit cost is an average value calculated on the basis of the entire series of preceding higher values.

Specific applications of the LC approach to the different manufacturing processes should be carried out with appropriate caution, whenever possible on the basis of robust statistical data, of experience on similar processes and considering all practical factors driving the actual path of manufacturing time reduction. The same approach can be extended, under case-specific conditions, to certain non-manufacturing processes. For example, in the software development area, Londeix (see Bibliography) mentions the Norden learning function p(t) indicating the effectiveness of a software project team.

Also technological upgrades may have a cumulative effect on cost reduction in parallel to the effect of learning. This upgrade may also extend to the entire organization managing the rationalization of manufacturing processes.

A typical manufacturing process may comprise machining operations and assembling or disassembling operations, in different proportions between different processes. In the assembling and disassembling phases of the process, which are typically manual, there is a potential chance for learning and, therefore, a significant reduction of time; in machining operations, the nature of processes inherently prevents all benefits from learning. If the proportion of assembling or disassembling operations is lesser, the reduction of average times becomes less relevant; conversely, if such proportion increases, although with extreme variations from one process to another, the adaptability of operators to these processes shows a great impact on the reduction of manufacturing time.

If new operational procedures and devices are introduced during a series production, this may significantly affect the time reduction curve. Care should, therefore, be taken in extending the time reduction approach to other situations. For example, introducing new machinery, rationalizing the equipment design and simplifying the working processes through technical modifications may accelerate the time reduction, in parallel with the learning process.

When series production is interrupted and resumed, unit cost is often higher than the level achieved before the interruption. Similarly, there is evidence that knowledge acquired through learning by doing depreciates: recent output rates may be a more important predictor of current production than cumulative output. Theoretical studies and simulation results have also indicated that this phenomenon, referred to as 'organizational forgetting', has implications for planning and scheduling.

The Effect of Production Breaks

The stability of production lines can be another aspect of possible effectiveness enhancement. Production breaks may take place as a result of delays in the production programme (budgetary or technical), time intervals between consecutive orders, or labour disputes. They may also result from design changes requiring shutdowns of production lines to introduce new tools and equipment or a new configuration, or from unpredicted recalls requiring repairs for previously produced items. The amount of lost learning depends on how long production lines experience breaks.

Cumulative Average Unit Cost Learning Curve and Unit Cost Learning Curve

There are two different learning curve models. A team of researchers at Stanford developed the approach referred to as the Incremental Unit Time (or Cost) Model or Crawford's Model. The original model had been developed by T. P. Wright in 1936 and is referred to as the Cumulative Average Model or Wright's Model.

The cumulative average unit cost technique is used to anticipate the average unit production cost for the total production programme as of the end of a certain time frame or extended production series, with respect to the average unit cost computed for an initial set of units.

According to Wright's law, if production quantity doubles, all other conditions remaining unchanged, the average direct labour time to manufacture each unit in the series will be reduced by a factor r between 0 and 1. If t_n denotes the average unit production time in a series of n units and t_{2n} denotes the average unit production time in a series of 2n units, the following equation is valid:

$$t_{2n} = r * t_n$$

The relationship between t_n and n is commonly called the learning curve, although in principle it should be drawn as a dotted line, since the abscissa *n* has only integer values.

The unit cost learning curve is based on three principles:

- The learning curve factor (for example, 80 per cent, as originally reported by T.P. Wright, or a different value) is mathematically applied as a decimal equivalent (namely 0.80).

- The 'double octave' principle is applicable, namely succeeding intervals between series production units, after the first unit, are always double the prior interval; if the learning curve impact after the initial production unit affects the 2nd unit, next intervals will be defined by the 4th unit, the 8th unit, the 16th unit and so on.

- The expected cost of each subsequent interval unit will be determined by multiplying the cost of the previous interval unit by the learning curve factor; for example, if one were to apply an 80 per cent learning curve factor to the aforesaid 'double octave' pattern, the cost of the 2nd unit would be 80 per cent of that of the first (initial) production unit, the cost of the 4th production unit would be 80 per cent of that of the 2nd unit, the cost of the 8th production unit would be 80 per cent of that of the 4th unit, and so on.

The Learning Curve from the Mathematical Perspective

UNIT COST FORMULA

Learning effects in manufacturing take place for an individual or an organization on the basis of the number of units manufactured.

Table A1.1 below applies for an 80 per cent learning rate, when 10 hours are required to manufacture the first unit.

Table A1.1   Unit, cumulative and average labour hours for an 80 per cent learning rate and 10 labour hours for the first unit

No. of unit	Unit direct labour hours	Cumulative direct labour hours	Average direct labour hours
1	10.00	10.00	10.00
2	8.00	18.00	9.00
4	6.40 (6 h 24 min)	31.42 (31 h 24 min)	7.85 (7 h 51 min)
8	5.12 (5 h 7 min)	53.46 (53 h 27 min)	6.68 (6 h 42 min)
16	4.09 (4 h 5 min)	89.20 (89 h 12 min)	5.57 (5 h 35 min)
32	3.28 (3 h 17 min)	146.79 (146 h 48 min)	4.59 (4 h 36 min)
64	2.62 (2 h 37 min)	239.24 (239 h 15 min)	3.74 (3 h 45 min)

The analytical expression of the learning curve can be drawn from the assumptions made.

Let:

x = number of unit;

t_x = number of direct labour hours to manufacture the xth unit;

t_1 = number of direct labour hours to manufacture the first unit;

r = learning curve factor in decimal form (for example: 0.90 if the learning rate is 90 per cent)

Direct labour hours for a given unit can be expressed by:

$$t_x = t_1 r^a \qquad \text{where:} \qquad x = 2^a$$

For values of a ranging from 0 upwards, we have:

$$t_x = t_1 r^0 \qquad \text{where:} \qquad x = 2^0 = 1$$

$$t_x = t_1 r^1 \qquad\qquad\qquad x = 2^1 = 2$$

$$t_x = t_1 r^2 \qquad\qquad\qquad x = 2^2 = 4$$

$$t_x = t_1 r^3 \qquad\qquad\qquad x = 2^3 = 8$$

Taking common logarithms, we obtain:

$$\log t_x = \log t_1 + a \log r \qquad \text{where:} \qquad \log x = a \log 2$$

hence the explicit expression of a:

$$a = \frac{\log t_x - \log t_1}{\log r} \qquad\qquad a = \frac{\log x}{\log 2}$$

$$\frac{\log t_x - \log t_1}{\log r} = \frac{\log x}{\log 2}$$

$$\log t_x - \log t_1 = \log r \, \frac{\log x}{\log 2}$$

Let: $n = \dfrac{\log r}{\log 2}$

$$\log t_x - \log t_1 = n \log x$$

$$\frac{t_x}{t_1} = x^n$$

$$t_x = t_1 x^n$$

The validity of learning curve information can be extended to the estimation of labour costs by multiplying the number of hours times the applicable labour rate.

The cost of a specific sequential unit in a production lot is:

$$C_x = C_1 \left(x^{\log r / \log 2} \right)$$

where:

C_x = cost of xth sequential unit assessed in production lot

C_1 = cost of initial (base) unit, or first unit in sequence

x = sequence number of units

r = learning curve factor

EXAMPLE OF UNIT COST LEARNING CURVE CALCULATION

By means of the foregoing equation, the values of unit direct labour hours in the table above can be calculated for each number of unit, assuming: $t_1 = 10$, $r = 0.8$.

For example, for the 8th unit the number of direct hours required will be:

$$t_8 = 10 \, (8)^{\log 0.8 / \log 2} = 10 \, (8)^{-0.322} = 5.12 \text{ hours}$$

CUMULATIVE AVERAGE UNIT COST FORMULA

Suppose a lot of N units is to be manufactured. If $t_x = t_1 x^n$ is the number of direct hours required to manufacture the xth unit, the sum of t_x values gives the cumulative number of direct hours required to manufacture all the N units in the lot:

$$T_N = t_1 + t_2 + \dots + t_N = \sum_{x=1}^{N} t_x$$

Replacing this sum with an integral, the cumulative number of direct hours can be approximated as follows:

$$T_N \approx t_1 \left[\frac{N^{n+1}}{n+1} \right]$$

This expression, divided by N, gives an approximation of the cumulative average number of direct hours:

$$\overline{T}_N \approx \frac{T_N}{N} \approx t_1 \frac{N^n}{n+1}$$

The cumulative average unit cost of each element in the production sequence C_i can be expressed as a function of the direct labour rate LR, direct material cost DM and overhead (in percentage OH vs. LR):

$$C_i = \overline{T}_N (LR) + DM + \overline{T}_N (LR) (OH)$$

and therefore:

$$C_i = t_1 \frac{N^n}{n+1} (LR) (1 + OH) + DM$$

EXAMPLE OF CUMULATIVE AVERAGE UNIT COST LEARNING CURVE CALCULATION

The application of Cumulative Average Unit Cost formula can be shown by a typical example which considers a number of N = 32 units to be manufactured. Let, in this didactic example, the labour rate be LR = £/h 90, the direct material unit cost DM = £1,000, the overhead percentage OH/LR = 90 per cent. Suppose t_1 = 100 direct labour hours for the first unit and r = 0.8 (80 per cent learning curve).

The cumulative average unit cost of each element in the production sequence is given by:

$$C_i = 100 \; \frac{32^{-0.322}}{-0.322 + 1} \; (90) \, (1.90) + 1{,}000 = £9{,}262$$

APPLICATION OF LEARNING CURVES IN A PRE-SERIES CASE

The application of the Unit Cost approach may be appropriate in negotiating the learning curve values for Full Rate Production contracts, pursuant to analysis of the manufacturing progress function for the pre-series units. The application of the Wright's approach will be considered for an extended series production.

Suppose the pre-series contract requires 32 'first article' units. The learning curve analysis for each pre-series unit will be based on labour hours t_x, obtained from actual manufacturing data (scatter plots) for the individual units during the pre-series phase:

$$t_{x2} = t_{x1} \, (X_2^{\, \log S / \log 2})$$

$$\log t_{x2} = \log t_{x1} + (\log X_2) \, (\log S / \log 2)$$

$$\log S = \frac{(\log 2) \, (\log t_{x2} - \log t_{x1})}{\log X_2}$$

hence the learning curve factor S, from known values of t_x, and $\log 2 = 0.30103$.

For example, determine the learning curve factor S from the following sets of values:

1. $t_{x1} = 4 \, h$ $t_{x2} = 3.75$ (3 h 45 min) $X_2 = 2 \Rightarrow$ $\log S = -0.02803$ $S = 0.9375$

2. $t_{x1} = 4 \, h$ $t_{x2} = 3.25$ (3 h 15 min) $X_2 = 4 \Rightarrow$ $\log S = -0.04509$ $S = 0.9014$

3. $t_{x1} = 4 \, h$ $t_{x2} = 2.50$ (2 h 30 min) $X_2 = 8 \Rightarrow$ $\log S = -0.06804$ $S = 0.8550$

4. $t_{x1} = 4 \, h$ $t_{x2} = 2.10$ (2 h 6 min) $X_2 = 16 \Rightarrow$ $\log S = -0.06996$ $S = 0.8512$

5. $t_{x1} = 4 \, h$ $t_{x2} = 1.25$ (1 h 15 min) $X_2 = 32 \Rightarrow$ $\log S = -0.10103$ $S = 0.7924$

Table A1.2 presents the complete set of calculations for the learning curve factor S, leading to the following final result:

$$\sum_{X_2 = 2}^{X_2 = 32} S = 26.2254$$

Table A1.2   Calculations for the learning curve factor

X_2	t_{x1}	t_{x2}	$\log X_2$	$\log t_{x1}$	$\log t_{x2}$	$\log S$	S
2	4	**3.75**	**0.30103**	**0.60206**	**0.57403**	**-0.02803**	**0.9375**
3	4	3.60	0.47712	0.60206	0.55630	-0.02887	0.9375
4	4	**3.25**	**0.60206**	**0.60206**	**0.51188**	**-0.04509**	**0.9014**
5	4	3.33	0.69897	0.60206	0.52244	-0.03429	0.9241
6	4	3.25	0.77815	0.60206	0.51188	-0.03489	0.9228
7	4	2.33	0.84510	0.60206	0.36736	-0.08360	0.8249
8	4	**2.50**	**0.90309**	**0.60206**	**0.39794**	**-0.06804**	**0.8550**
9	4	2.40	0.95424	0.60206	0.38021	-0.06999	0.8512
10	4	2.25	1.00000	0.60206	0.35218	-0.07522	0.8410
11	4	2.10	1.04139	0.60206	0.32222	-0.08089	0.8301
12	4	2.20	1.07918	0.60206	0.34242	-0.07242	0.8464
13	4	2.15	1.11394	0.60206	0.33244	-0.07286	0.8455
14	4	2.30	1.14613	0.60206	0.36173	-0.06312	0.8647
15	4	2.00	1.17609	0.60206	0.30103	-0.07705	0.8374
16	4	**2.10**	**1.20412**	**0.60206**	**0.32222**	**-0.06996**	**0.8512**
17	4	1.90	1.23045	0.60206	0.27875	-0.07910	0.8335
18	4	1.80	1.25527	0.60206	0.25527	-0.08316	0.8257
19	4	1.85	1.27875	0.60206	0.26717	-0.07884	0.8340
20	4	2.35	1.30103	0.60206	0.37107	-0.05345	0.8842
21	4	1.90	1.32222	0.60206	0.27875	-0.07361	0.8441
22	4	1.70	1.34242	0.60206	0.23045	-0.08333	0.8254
23	4	1.65	1.36173	0.60206	0.21748	-0.08502	0.8222
24	4	1.60	1.38021	0.60206	0.20412	-0.08679	0.8189
25	4	1.55	1.39794	0.60206	0.19033	-0.08866	0.8153
26	4	1.50	1.41497	0.60206	0.17609	-0.09062	0.8117
27	4	1.70	1.43136	0.60206	0.23045	-0.07815	0.8353
28	4	1.45	1.44716	0.60206	0.16137	-0.09167	0.8097
29	4	1.40	1.46240	0.60206	0.14613	-0.09385	0.8057
30	4	1.35	1.47712	0.60206	0.13033	-0.09614	0.8014
31	4	1.30	1.49136	0.60206	0.11394	-0.09853	0.7970
32	4	**1.25**	**1.50515**	**0.60206**	**0.09691**	**-0.10103**	**0.7924**

Hence: $S = \dfrac{26.2254}{31} = 0.8460 \approx 0.85 \quad = 85\%$

Appendix 2
Further considerations on System Effectiveness and Life Cycle Cost

Calculation of System Effectiveness

Let us consider a very simple (and didactically useful) case study, showing how numerical values (entirely hypothetical) of System Effectiveness can be calculated in practice.

Our system consists of a vehicle for emergency use, with its radio communication equipment.

The mission of the system is to transport personnel in charge of emergency, with equipment needed, on random call, to the sites requiring a mission within a range of one-half hour.

The following assumptions are considered:

1. A single vehicle at a time may respond to a call. If the vehicle is not able to respond (for example, if it is undergoing maintenance), no mission is carried out.

2. The vehicle is required to reach its operational site in 30 minutes.

3. No maintenance or repair operations on radio equipment are possible on the move.

4.   The mission fails if the vehicle cannot reach the operational site.

For purpose of the model formulation, the following system states are identified:

- State 1   Vehicle operational, radio equipment operable

- State 2   Vehicle operational, radio equipment inoperable

- State 3   Vehicle not in operational condition.

In order for the relationship

$$SE = A_0 * D_0 * C$$

to be applicable, factors in 2nd member are defined as follows:

Availability – Three-element row vector:

$$A_0 = [a_1, a_2, a_3]$$

where a_i is the probability that the vehicle will be in State i at the time of call.

Dependability – 3 . 3 square matrix:

$$D_0 = \begin{bmatrix} d_{11} & d_{12} & d_{13} \\ d_{21} & d_{22} & d_{23} \\ d_{31} & d_{32} & d_{33} \end{bmatrix}$$

being d_{ij} the probability that if the vehicle is in State i at the time of call it will complete its mission in State j.

Capability – Three-element column vector:

$$C = \begin{bmatrix} c_1 \\ c_2 \\ c_3 \end{bmatrix}$$

where c_i is the probability that, if the vehicle arrives at its destination in State i, the mission can be successfully completed. For multi-capability systems, C would be a multi-column matrix.

DEFINITION OF MODEL ELEMENTS

Let us suppose that, on the basis of past experience, the average time between maintenance operations (both preventive and due to failures) for this type of vehicle is 80 hours and the average duration of a maintenance operation (taking into account complex operations and other factors) is 2 hours. In addition, concerning the radio equipment, let the following values be applicable: mean time between maintenance 400 hours; mean time to repair 2 hours.

The elements of Availability can be, therefore, determined as follows:

a_1 = P (vehicle operable) * P(radio equipment operable) =

$$a_1 = \left[\frac{80}{80 + 2} \right] \left[\frac{400}{400 + 2} \right] = 0.97$$

a_2 = P (vehicle operable) * P (radio equipment inoperable) =

$$a_2 = \left[\frac{80}{80 + 2} \right] \left[\frac{2}{400 + 2} \right] = 0.005$$

$$a_3 = \text{P (vehicle inoperable)} = \left[\frac{2}{80 + 2} \right] = 0.024$$

Let us consider Dependability next. Here we assume that the time between failures of the radio equipment is exponentially distributed with a mean of 400 hours and that the probability that the vehicle on the move will not successfully accomplish its mission is 0.08. Therefore, the following cases are identified:

1. the initial system state is State 1

2. the initial system state is State 2

3. the initial system state is State 3

In case (1):

d_{11} = P (vehicle accomplishes mission) * P (radio equipment remains operable)

$$= (1 - 0.08)\, e^{\frac{-1/2}{400}} = 0.919$$

d_{12} = P (vehicle accomplishes mission) * P (radio equipment fails on the move)

$$= (1 - 0.08) * (1 - e^{\frac{-1/2}{400}}) = 0.001$$

d_{13} = P (vehicle does not accomplish mission) = 0.08

In case (2):

d_{21} = 0 (the radio equipment cannot be repaired on the move)

d_{22} = P (vehicle accomplishes mission) = 0.92

d_{23} = P (vehicle does not accomplish mission) = 0.08

In case (3):

d_{31} = d_{32} = 0 because the mission will not start

d_{33} = 1 (this means that, if the vehicle is not operable, it will remain not operable with reference to a particular mission)

Finally, as regards Capability, technical assessments and past experience determine that the probability of successful mission is c_i if the system is in State i at the time of arrival at its destination:

$c_1 = 0.90$　　　　　$c_2 = 0.85$　　　　　$c_3 = 0$

DETERMINATION OF SYSTEM EFFECTIVENESS

The final result of our calculation is the following:

$$SE = \begin{bmatrix} 0.97 & 0.005 & 0.024 \end{bmatrix} \begin{bmatrix} 0.919 & 0.001 & 0.08 \\ 0 & 0.92 & 0.08 \\ 0 & 0 & 1 \end{bmatrix} \begin{bmatrix} 0.90 \\ 0.85 \\ 0 \end{bmatrix}$$

$$SE = 0.8772 * 0.8455 = 0.7417$$

This means that the system has a probability of about 74 per cent of successfully completing its mission. The value we obtain allows us to determine whether improvements are necessary. Possible alternatives will be evaluated on the basis of SE value, as a function of varying numerical values in the SE equation.

Selection Between Two Alternatives

We now consider an example of selection between two alternatives on the basis of LCC. In this simple case, our 'system' is represented by a vehicle (this example may be obviously adapted to more general cases).

Let's suppose that our organization receives two quotations for the purchase of 500 vehicles for use in our warehouses. Both vehicles A and B are fully compliant with our requirements, but vehicle B has a unit purchase cost of £6,000 more than vehicle A.

We need this vehicle to operate for a total of 6 years, 750 hours per year:

500 vehicles * 750 * 6 = 2,250,000 total hours

In the case of vehicle A the following values apply: MTBF = 60 hours, MTTR = 3.5 hours for each maintenance operation, personnel cost £53/hour, material cost £150 in each operation. Therefore:

$$\frac{2,250,000}{60} = 37,500 \text{ maintenance operations}$$

37,500 * 3.5 * 53 = £6,956,250 personnel cost

37,500 * 150 = £5,625,000 material cost

hence a total cost of £12,581,250.

The values for vehicle B are MTBF = 110 hours, MTTR = 2.8 hours for each maintenance operation, personnel cost £53/hour, material cost £175 in each operation. Therefore:

$$\frac{2,250,000}{110} = 20,455 \text{ maintenance operations}$$

20,455 * 2.8 * 53 = £3,035,522 personnel cost

20,455 * 175 = £3,579,625 material cost

and adding the purchase cost difference of the 500 vehicles:

500 * 6,000 = £3,000,000

hence a total cost (calculated on the whole of the 500 vehicles) of £9,615,147, lower than that of vehicle A by £2,966,103, which amounts to about £6,000 per vehicle.

Now, we are going to approach a *sensitivity analysis* considering the uncertainty on the parameters of reliability and maintainability of vehicle B, with no variation in those of vehicle A. With respect to the aforesaid 'nominal' values, let's consider MTBF values equal to 60 per cent, 75 per cent and 90 per cent and MTTR values equal to 110 per cent, 125 per cent and 140 per cent. Let's make only MTBF variable with no variation of MTTR and of overall service hours.

Table A2.1   Sensitivity analysis with variable MTBF

%	MTBF nominal	MTBF calculated	Maintenance operations
60	110	66.0	34,090.9
75	110	82.6	27,272.7
90	110	99.0	22,727.3

Table A2.1a   Calculation of total labour cost

Maintenance operations	MTTR	Hourly rate	Total cost
34,090.9	2.8	53	£5,059,090
27,272.7	2.8	53	£4,047,269
22,727.3	2.8	53	£3,372,731

Table A2.1b   Calculation of total material cost

Maintenance operations	Cost of spares per operation	Total material costs
34,090.9	175	£5,965,908
27,272.7	175	£4,772,723
22,727.3	175	£3,977,278

Table A2.1c   Calculation of total cost

Cost of labour	Cost of materials	Purchase cost difference	Total cost
£5,059,090	£5,965,908	3,000,000	£14,024,998
£4,047,269	£4,772,723	3,000,000	£11,819,992
£3,372,731	£3,977,278	3,000,000	£10,350,009

Let's now suppose that MTTR varies being MTBF constant. Sensitivity analysis is repeated accordingly.

Table A2.2   Sensitivity analysis with variable MTTR

%	MTTR nominal	MTTR calculated
110	2.8	3.08
125	2.8	3.50
140	2.8	3.92

Table A2.2a   Calculation of total labour cost

Maintenance operations	MTTR calculated	Hourly cost	Total cost
20,455	3.08	53	£3,339,074
20,455	3.50	53	£3,794,403
20,455	3.92	53	£4,249,731

Table A2.2b   Calculation of total cost

Cost of personnel	Cost of materials	Purchase cost difference	Total cost
£3,339,074	£3,579,625	3,000,000	£9,918,699
£3,794,403	£3,579,625	3,000,000	£10,374,028
£4,249,731	£3,579,625	3,000,000	£10,829,356

On the basis of the aforementioned values, we can conclude that:

- the maintainability variation has no influence on the decision in favour of vehicle B;

- the reliability variation only influences if the MTBF value of vehicle B is reduced to about 70 per cent of nominal value.

Evaluation of System Economic Life

In several engineering problems, the evaluation of system *economic life* is a major economic issue, from the point of view of its applications in optimizing the LCC (in compliance with system life cycle planning) and in looking for alternative solutions to arrive at the most suitable configuration(s) on the basis of LCC.

Below we will discuss how to evaluate (in theory) a system economic life, taking care of the following necessary information: acquisition cost; annual per cent value decrease; annual utilisation and support costs; cost discounting rate.

Let's consider the following data (these values are only quantitatively indicative): acquisition cost C = £240,000; annual value decrease 20 per cent; Utilization and Support costs for the first year £30,000, annual linear increase £12,000; cost discounting rate 10 per cent (in decimal form 0.1).

First of all, it should be taken into account that the annual per cent value decrease of 20 per cent of the system economic value means, for instance, that at the end of the first service year the value will be the following:

$C_1 = 0.8 * £240,000 = £192,000$

and at the end of the second year:

$C_2 = 0.8 * £192,000 = £153,600$

We now calculate the net annual value for the first year (costs are indicated with a minus sign), using standard formulae from financial analysis, being:

$$A_1 = -C \frac{i(1+i)^n}{(1+i)^n - 1} = -240,000 \frac{0.1(1+0.1)^1}{(1+0.1)^1 - 1} = -£264,000$$

the discounted cost;

$$V_1 = +C_1 \frac{i}{(1+i)^n - 1} = +192,000 \frac{0.1}{(1+0.1)^1 - 1}$$

the discounted value. If we consider the Utilization and Support costs for the first year, S = - £30.000, the net annual value will be given by:

$$\Delta V_1 = -264.000 + 192.000 - 30.000 = -£102.000$$

If we repeat the same procedure for the subsequent years until the sixth year, we obtain the values in Table A2.3.

Table A2.3   Evaluation of system economic life

Year	1	2	3	4	5	6
C	- 240,000					
A	- 264,000	- 138,290	- 96,500	- 75,720	- 63,310	- 55,100
V_1	+192,000					
$0.8 * V_{n-1}$		+153,600	+122,880	+98,300	+78,640	+62,910
PV V_n	+192,000	+73,140	+37,120	+21,180	+12,880	+8,150
S	- 30,000	- 30,000	- 30,000	- 30,000	- 30,000	- 30,000
ΔS	0	- 5,710	- 11,240	- 16,570	- 21,720	- 26,690
ΔV	−102,000	−100,860	−100,630	−101,110	−102,150	−103,640

Specifically, it should be noted that the values tabulated for ΔS each year can be obtained from the following formula:

$$\Delta S = -12,000 \frac{A}{G}$$

where

$$\frac{A}{G} = \frac{1}{i} - \frac{n}{(1+i)^n - 1}$$

The net annual values ΔV tabulated give us the indication that the net annual value is '*less negative*' for a duration of *three* years: this is therefore the *optimum economic life* of our system, in accordance with the limits within which our hypotheses remain valid.

The Economic Life and the System Replacement Problem

The estimated value of the optimum economic life of a generic system makes it possible, for instance, to determine at which point in time it is convenient to replace the existing system, in accordance with exclusively economic criteria, with a new system suitable for the same 'operational profile'. In order to achieve this goal, the procedure can be different from the aforementioned method based on annual values. The feasible alternative is based on present economic values.

We can calculate both the optimum replacement period for the system and the life cycle duration for the alternative system by evaluating the Net Present Value (NPV) of each feasible combination of the two life cycles, then choosing the *minimum cost NPV* (or else, the *maximum NPV of net incomes*), having noted that this procedure is in principle applicable only if the two systems have equal lives. As a consequence, the first basic problem derives from the different combinations between the durations of the life cycles of the existing system and the alternative system: for example, one year plus four years, versus three years plus five years. Therefore, we can conclude that we have to compare the NPV on a total, respectively, of five and eight years, hence 40 combinations in total. This complication can be overcome by assuming an *infinite* series of replacements, or, for instance, an existing system for one year of life and infinite replacements with alternative systems, each one for four years of life. This assumption can be compared to assuming a system with three years of life and infinite replacements with alternative systems having five years of life each. The utilization of infinite series is an important method to determine the optimum system life duration: in this case, each combination has an overall life cycle of infinite duration and, therefore, the comparative criteria based on NPV is correctly applicable and, furthermore, the analytical process is greatly simpler.

Now, the practical applications of these discussions can be better explained with a numerical example appropriate to solve the following problems:

1. beginning from now, how long is it convenient to wait before replacing the existing system with an alternative system?

2. if there is no replacement, what is the optimal remaining life of the current system?

3. what is the optimal life cycle duration of the alternative system?

Let us suppose that the data in Table A2.4 are given and that the applicable rate is $i = 15$ per cent.

In the calculation of NPV for the existing system, let us consider tentative values of its remaining life N_1, for instance from 0 to 4 years. As regards the alternative system, its NPV is calculated for an infinite series of life cycles, each one for a tentative duration N_2 from 1 to 5 years; the corresponding payments are all changed into overall sums located at the end of each life cycle, representing a periodic infinite series.

Table A2.4   System economic life

System data	Existing	Alternative
Present market value	$V_1 = £160,000$	
Purchase cost		$C_2 = £260,000$
Annual value decrease	$\Delta V_1 = 20$ per cent	$\Delta V_2 = 20$ per cent
Constant amount of annual Operation and Support costs	$A_1 = £72,000$	$A_2 = £60,000$
Linear annual increase of Operation and Support costs	$\Delta A_1 = £16,000$	$\Delta A_2 = £13,000$

Now we calculate the commercial values of existing system for N_1 variable from 1 to 4 (note that for $N_1 = 0$ the value is £160,000), decreasing each year by a factor of 20 per cent:

- for $N_1 = 1$ $V_{1,1} = V_1 - \Delta V_1 = £128,000$

- for $N_1 = 2$ $V_{1,2} = V_{1,1} * 0,8 = £102,400$

- for $N_1 = 3$ $V_{1,3} = V_{1,2} * 0,8 = £81,920$

- for $N_1 = 4$ $V_{1,4} = V_{1,3} * 0,8 = £65,536$

The corresponding present values are calculated by dividing the single values found by the term $1{,}15^{N_1}$:

- for $N_1 = 1$ $PV_{1,1} = \dfrac{V_{1,1}}{1.15} = \dfrac{128{,}000}{1.15} = £111{,}304$

- for $N_1 = 2$ $PV_{1,2} = \dfrac{V_{1,2}}{1.15^2} = \dfrac{102{,}400}{1.15^2} = £77{,}429$

- for $N_1 = 3$ $PV_{1,3} = \dfrac{V_{1,3}}{1.15^3} = \dfrac{81{,}920}{1.15^3} = £53{,}864$

- for $N_1 = 4$ $PV_{1,4} = \dfrac{V_{1,4}}{1.15^4} = \dfrac{65.536}{1.15^4} = £37{,}470$

In the following step, we calculate the present values of the constant part of annual Utilization and Support costs, which we obtain by multiplying the value given $A_1 = £72{,}000$ by the discounting factor

$$\frac{1.15^{N_1} - 1}{0.15 * 1.15^{N_1}}$$

for N_1 variable from 1 to 4 (obviously, for $N_1 = 0$, the value is 0):

- for $N_1 = 1$ $A_{1,1} = 72{,}000 * 0.869565 = £62{,}609$

- for $N_1 = 2$ $A_{1,2} = 72{,}000 * 1.625709 = £117{,}051$

- for $N_1 = 3$ $A_{1,3} = 72{,}000 * 2.283225 = £164{,}392$

- for $N_1 = 4$ $A_{1,4} = 72{,}000 * 2.854978 = £205{,}558$

Subsequently, we calculate the present values of linear increases of annual Utilization and Support costs, that can be obtained by multiplying the value given $\Delta A_1 = £16{,}000$ by the discounting factor

$$\frac{1}{0.15}\left[\frac{1.15^{N_1} - 1}{0.15 * 1.15^{N_1}} - \frac{N_1}{1.15^{N_1}} \right]$$

for N_1 variable from 1 to 4 (this time, we have zero values both for $N_1 = 0$ and – as can be easily seen – for $N_1 = 1$):

- for $N_1 = 1$ $\Delta A_{1,1} = 0$

- for $N_1 = 2$ $\Delta A_{1,2} = 16{,}000 * 0.75614 = £12{,}098$

- for $N_1 = 3$ $\Delta A_{1,3} = 16{,}000 * 2.07118 = £33{,}138$

- for $N_1 = 4$ $\Delta A_{1,4} = 16{,}000 * 3.78644 = £60{,}582$

On the basis of our calculations, it is possible to determine as a whole the system NPV as algebraic sum of values found for N_1 variable from 1 to 4 (still remaining a zero value for $N_1 = 0$), or: $NPV_1 = -V_1 + PV_{1,N1} - A_{1,N1} - \Delta A_{1,N1}$.

We obtain therefore:

- for $N_1 = 1$ $NPV_{1,1} = -160{,}000 + 111{,}304 - 62{,}609 - 0 = -£111{,}305$

- for $N_1 = 2$ $NPV_{1,2} = -160{,}000 + 77{,}429 - 117{,}051 - 12{,}098 = -£211{,}720$

- for $N_1 = 3$ $NPV_{1,3} = -160{,}000 + 53{,}864 - 164{,}392 - 33{,}138 = -£303{,}666$

- for $N_1 = 4$ $NPV_{1,4} = -160{,}000 + 37{,}470 - 205{,}558 - 60{,}582 = -£388{,}670$

As regards the alternative system, confirming our anticipations, we will calculate our NPV for an infinite series of life cycles, each one for a tentative duration N_2 from 1 to 5 years. Corresponding payments can be transformed into lump sums by introducing the term $i_2 = (1 + i)^{N2} - 1$, assuming the following values:

- for $N_2 = 1$ $i_{2,1} = 1 + 0.15 - 1 = 0.15$

- for $N_2 = 2$ $i_{2,2} = (1 + 0.15)^2 - 1 = 0.3225$

- for $N_2 = 3$ $i_{2,3} = (1 + 0.15)^3 - 1 = 0.5209$

- for $N_2 = 4$ $i_{2,2} = (1 + 0.15)^4 - 1 = 0.7490$

- for $N_2 = 5$ $i_{2,5} = (1 + 0.15)^5 - 1 = 1.0113$

Let us now calculate the overall cost, year by year (hence for N_2 variable from 1 to 5), for the system (£260,000) and for the infinite replacement series. In the latter case, on the basis of the aforesaid considerations, we apply the usual relationship by which the overall present value P of a periodic series of payments is expressed, being A the amount of each payment, if the number of payments tends to ∞:

$$\frac{P}{A} = \frac{(1 + i_2)^n - 1}{(1 + i_2)^n * i_2}$$

In our case, assuming $n \Rightarrow \infty$, the second member becomes:

$$\frac{P}{A} = \frac{1}{i_2}$$

As a result, the values of $C_2 + \dfrac{C_2}{i_2}$ will be the following:

- for $N_2 = 1$ $260{,}000 + \dfrac{260{,}000}{0.15} = \text{£}1{,}993{,}333$

- for $N_2 = 2$ $260{,}000 + \dfrac{260{,}000}{0.3225} = \text{£}1{,}066{,}202$

- for $N_2 = 3$ $260{,}000 + \dfrac{260{,}000}{0.5209} = \text{£}759{,}136$

- for $N_2 = 4$ $260{,}000 + \dfrac{260{,}000}{0.7490} = \text{£}607{,}129$

- for $N_2 = 5$ $260{,}000 + \dfrac{260{,}000}{1.0113} = \text{£}517{,}095$

Subsequently, we determine the market values of alternative system by varying N_2 (for $N_2 = 0$ the value is £260,000), declining each year, in accordance with our data, by a factor of 20 per cent. For each value found we apply, respectively, the same expression of infinite series that has been already used:

- for $N_2 = 1$ $V_{2,1} = C_2 - \Delta V_2 = \text{£}208{,}000$

  $$\frac{V_{2,1}}{i_{2,1}} = \frac{208{,}000}{0.15} = \text{£}1{,}386{,}667$$

- for $N_2 = 2$ $V_{2,2} = V_{2,1} * 0.8 = \text{£}166{,}400$

  $$\frac{V_{2,2}}{i_{2,2}} = \frac{166{,}400}{0.3225} = \text{£}515{,}969$$

- for $N_2 = 3$ $V_{2,3} = V_{2,2} * 0.8 = \text{£}133{,}120$

$$\frac{V_{2,3}}{i_{2,3}} = \frac{133,120}{0.5209} = £255,558$$

- for $N_2 = 4$ $V_{2,4} = V_{2,3} * 0.8 = £106,496$

$$\frac{V_{2,4}}{i_{2,4}} = \frac{106,496}{0.7490} = £142,184$$

- for $N_2 = 5$ $V_{2,5} = V_{2,4} * 0.8 = £85,197$

$$\frac{V_{2,4}}{i_{2,4}} = \frac{85,197}{1.0113} = £84,245$$

In the following step we calculate the present values of the constant part of annual Utilization and Support costs, by multiplying the value given $A_2 = £60,000$ by the factor

$$\frac{1.15^{N_2} - 1}{0.15 * i_2}$$

for N_2 variable from 1 to 5:

- for $N_2 = 1$ $A_{2,1} = 60,000 * \dfrac{1.15 - 1}{0.15*0.15} = £400,000$

- for $N_2 = 2$ $A_{2,2} = 60,000 * \dfrac{1.15^2 - 1}{0.15*0.3225} = £400,000$

- for $N_2 = 3$ $A_{2,3} = 60,000 * \dfrac{1.15^3 - 1}{0.15*0.5209} = £400,000$

- for $N_2 = 4$ $A_{2,4} = 60,000 * \dfrac{1.15^4 - 1}{0.15*0.7490} = £400,000$

- for $N_2 = 5$ $A_{2,5} = 60,000 * \dfrac{1.15^5 - 1}{0.15*1.0113} = £400,000$

The next item of the procedure is the calculation of present values of linear increases of annual Utilization and Support costs, which we obtain by multiplying the value given $\Delta A_2 = £13,000$ by the factor

$$\frac{1}{i_2} * \frac{1}{0.15} \left[\frac{1.15^{N_2} - 1}{0.15} - N_2 \right]$$

hence:

- for $N_2 = 1$ $\Delta A_{2,1} = 13,000 * \dfrac{1}{0.15} * \dfrac{1}{0.15} \left[\dfrac{1.15 - 1}{0.15} - 1 \right] = 0$

- for $N_2 = 2$ $\Delta A_{2,2} = 13,000 * \dfrac{1}{0.3225} * \dfrac{1}{0.15} \left[\dfrac{1.15^2 - 1}{0.15} - 2 \right]$

$$\Delta A_{2,2} = \text{£ } 40{,}310$$

- for $N_2 = 3$ $\Delta A_{2,3} = 13{,}000 * \dfrac{1}{0.5209} * \dfrac{1}{0.15} \left[\dfrac{1.15^3 - 1}{0.15} - 3 \right]$

$$\Delta A_{2,3} = \text{£}78{,}614$$

- for $N_2 = 4$ $\Delta A_{2,4} = 13{,}000 * \dfrac{1}{0.7490} * \dfrac{1}{0.15} \left[\dfrac{1.15^4 - 1}{0.15} - 4 \right]$

$$\Delta A_{2,4} = \text{£}114{,}943$$

- for $N_2 = 5$ $\Delta A_{2,5} = 13{,}000 * \dfrac{1}{1.0113} * \dfrac{1}{0.15} \left[\dfrac{1.15^5 - 1}{0.15} - 5 \right]$

$$\Delta A_{2,5} = \text{£}149{,}319$$

Consequently the system NPV will be calculated as the algebraic sum of values found for N_2 variable from 1 to 5:

$$NPV_2 = - C_2 - \frac{C_2}{i_2} + \frac{V_2}{i_2} - A_{2, N2} - \Delta A_{2, N2}.$$

Therefore:

- for $N_2 = 1$ $NPV_{2,1} = -1{,}993{,}333 + 1{,}386{,}667 - 400{,}000 - 0 = -\text{£}1{,}006{,}666$

- for $N_2 = 2$ $NPV_{2,2} = -1{,}066{,}202 + 515{,}969 - 400{,}000 - 40{,}310 = -\text{£}990{,}543$

- for $N_2 = 3$ $NPV_{2,3} = -759{,}136 + 255{,}558 - 400{,}000 - 78{,}614 = -\text{£}982{,}192$

- for $N_2 = 4$ $NPV_{2,4} = -607{,}129 + 142{,}184 - 400{,}000 - 114{,}943 = -\text{£}979{,}888$

- for $N_2 = 5$ $NPV_{2,5} = -517{,}095 + 84{,}245 - 400{,}000 - 149{,}319 = -\text{£}982{,}169$

Our previous calculations, finally, lead us to the results we wished to obtain, by adding the NPVs of the two systems, the existing and the alternative, for each combination of the values of remaining life N_1 of the existing system from 0 (in correspondence with the immediate replacement of the existing system) to 4 and of the life N_2 of the alternative system from 1 to 5.

In Table A2.5, we can see the recapitulation of the results coming from NPV sums, noting that for N_1 variable from 1 to 4 the values are corresponding to:

$$NPV_1 + NPV_2 \frac{1}{1,15^{N_1}}$$

Table A2.5   Results of NPV calculations

N_2 / N_1	1	2	3	4	5
0	-1,006,666	- 990,543	- 982,192	- 979,888	- 982,169
1	- 986,667	- 972,647	- 965,385	- 963,382	- 965,365
2	- 972,904	- 960,713	- 954,398	- 952,656	- 954,381
3	- 965,565	- 954,964	- 949,473	**-947,958**	- 949,458
4	- 964,235	- 955,016	- 950,241	- 948,924	- 950,228

Looking at the values in the table, we can observe that the *least negative* value is **– £ 947,958**, corresponding to the values **$N_1 = 3$** and **$N_2 = 4$**.

Taking into account this *minimum cost*, we can therefore find the answers to the initial questions:

1. beginning from this moment, it is convenient to replace the existing system with an alternative system after a period of 3 years;

2. in case the replacement does not take place, the remaining life of the existing system is 3 years;

3. the optimum life cycle duration of the alternative system is 4 years.

Additionally, on the basis of our results, for instance, it is possible to evaluate (still in terms of present value) the economic loss that would arise if the existing system should be replaced immediately ($N_1 = 0$) instead of the 3 years established ($N_1 = 3$), having fixed $N_2 = 4$:

- £979,888 + £947,958 = - £31,930

In this type of procedure it is necessary to consider that the purchase prices of the series of alternative systems are not constant, since they are increasing from one system to the subsequent, both as a result of the inflation and due to technological improvements. This occurs if we neglect the effect of *learning* in medium to large series production (see the previous Appendix on *learning curves*), which initially tends to significantly lowering the unit production costs. Let us suppose, for example, that all costs of alternative systems, inclusive of the purchase price, increase by a certain quantity each year: let r be its estimated value, referred to the unit. Therefore, if we indicate as n the number of years elapsing from a replacement to the subsequent, the periodic cost increment will be represented by the factor $(1 + r)^n$.

Hence, supposing that the annual increase percentage is 5 per cent and that the replacement occurs every 5 years, for each replacement the purchase cost will be higher by a factor of $1.05^5 = 1.2763$; consequently, if the first replacement costs £10,000, the next replacement occurring five years later will have an estimated cost of £12,763.

Bibliography

Blanchard, B.S. 1978. *Design and Manage to Life Cycle Cost*. Forest Grove: M/A Press.

Blanchard, B.S. and Fabrycky, W.J. 1990. *Systems Engineering and Analysis*. Upper Saddle River: Prentice Hall.

Blanchard, B.S. 2008. *Systems Engineering Management*. New York: J. Wiley & Sons.

Building Cost Information Service, British Standards Institution 2008. *Standardized Method of Life Cycle Costing for Construction Procurement*. London: BCIS/BSI.

Department of the Navy, United States of America 2003. *Operational Availability Handbook. A Practical Guide for Military Systems, Sub-Systems and Equipment*.

Emblemsvåg, J. 2003. *Life-Cycle Costing. Using Activity-Based Costing and Monte Carlo Methods to Manage Future Costs and Risks*. Hoboken: John Wiley & Sons.

Farr, J.V. 2011. *Systems Life Cycle Costing*. Boca Raton: CRC Press.

Federal Aviation Administration (FAA) 2002. *Life Cycle Cost Estimating Handbook*.

Garvey, P.R. 1999. *Probability Methods for Cost Uncertainty Analysis. A Systems Engineering Perspective*. New York: Marcel Dekker.

Hopkinson, M., Close, P., Hillson, D., and Ward, S. 2008. *'Prioritising Project Risks – A Short Guide to Useful Techniques'*. Princes Risborough: Association for Project Management.

Hulett, D. 2011. *Integrated Cost-Schedule Risk Analysis*. Farnham: Gower Publishing.

IEC 60300-3-3:2004. *Dependability Management Part 3-3: Application Guide – Life Cycle Costing*.

International Council on Systems Engineering 2007. *Systems Engineering Handbook*.

ISO/IEC 15288:2008. *Systems and Software Engineering – System Life Cycle Processes*.

Jones, C. 2012. *A Short History of the Lines of Code (LoC) Metric*. Providence: Capers Jones & Associates LLC.

Jones, C. 2012. *How Software Personnel Learn New Skills: An Evaluation of Modern Learning Methods*. Providence: Capers Jones & Associates LLC.

Jones, C. 2012. *Errors and Omissions in Software Historical Data: Separating Fact from Fiction*. Providence: Capers Jones & Associates LLC.

Londeix, B. 1987. *Cost Estimation for Software Development*. Wokingham: Addison Wesley.

McCormick, E.J. and Sanders, M.S. 1993. *Human Factors in Engineering and Design*. New York: McGraw-Hill.

National Aeronautics and Space Administration 2008. *NASA Cost Estimating Handbook*.

NATO 2007. *Publication ALCCP-1 - NATO Guidance on Life Cycle Costing*

NATO 2007. *Publication RTO TR-SAS-054 – Methods and Models for Life Cycle Costing*.

NATO 2009. *Publication RTO TR-SAS-069 – Code of Practice for Life Cycle Costing*.

Park, C.S. 2002. *Contemporary Engineering Economics*. Upper Saddle River: Prentice Hall.

Shermon, D. 2009. *Systems Cost Engineering – Program Affordability Management and Cost Control*. Farnham: Gower Publishing.

Society of Cost Estimating and Analysis (SCEA) 2003. *Cost Estimating Body of Knowledge (CEBoK)*.

Sommerville, I. 2011. *Software Engineering*. Boston: Addison-Wesley.

Stewart, R.D., Wyskida, R.M. and Johannes J.D. (Eds.) 1995. *Cost Estimator's Reference Manual*. New York: J. Wiley & Sons.

Thuesen, G.J., and Fabrycky W.J. 1993. *Engineering Economy*. Upper Saddle River: Prentice Hall.

US Air Force 2007. *Cost Risk and Uncertainty Handbook*.

Index